Life with Toddlers

3 Simple Strategies to Ease the Struggle and Raise Happy, Healthy Toddlers

Michelle Smith M.S., SLP

with Rita Chandler, Ph. D.

Cover design by Jerry Holguin and Chris Smith, cover photo courtesy of Gail Roberts.

Interior design, illustrations, and photos by Chris Smith.

Printed and bound in the United States of America

Second Edition

Put the essential 3 step "TAG" or Toddler ABC Guide© on your fridge, by going to www.LifeWithToddlers.com and clicking on the refrigerator icon to get a printable version.

"TAG" or Toddler ABC Guide©

Put this essential 3 step guide on your fridge.

A) What happens just before the behavior [what set it off]?

B) Clearly define behavior [hitting, biting, yelling, etc].

C) What is your reaction? It will:

      P - punish [stop] behavior
        or
      R - reinforce [continue] behavior

A) _____

B) _____

C) _____

    P = _____

    R = _____

Remember The Five Basics! Structure, Communication, Limits, Consistency, Guidance. Use these to set up "A" and "C" for success!

The Toddler ABC Guide© is explained in the book
"Life With Toddlers" by Michelle Smith.

Please visit www.LifeWithToddlers.com for more information.

For my sweet baby girls: Poppy, Mimi, and Wee.
For nearly a decade of toddler adventures...and for growing up so
beautiful, inside and out.

Contents

Acknowledgements

To Debbie Dodson, Miss Connie, and all the wonderful teachers at Crossing Point Christian School, thank you so much for letting me invade your space, take data, bombard you with questions, and enjoy your kids.

To Dr. Rita Chandler, for your endless patience with my eight million phone calls and emails, your terrific input on ABA, and your love for my girls – thank you. Love ya sis!

To Jerry Holguin, for your awesome work on the cover, and Gail Roberts and family for letting me use the image of your fantastic, dirty, covered-in-cake grandkids – thank you so much.

To my Poker Mommies – especially Amy (for listening to me rant for the last 8 years) – for your fabulous stories, tons of laughter, and lack of sympathy. You keep me grounded!

Most of all, for my husband. Chris, words just can't do it, honey. Every single day, you show me and the kids what true love is. I love you and will never be able to thank you enough for your love, support of this 8 year project, and help pushing it through. It wouldn't be out there without you.

Introduction: "Experts" can BITE me!

Okay. I've read them all. The how-to's, the why's, the try-it-this-way's. You know what I'm talking about. You pick up a book on toddlers or discipline, bound and determined to do as the experts say and end up with what they promise; a happy, loving, respectable little angel.

Well. While there seems to be plenty of letters behind the authors' names and a plethora of suggestions on what to do, let me tell you what's missing in all these books; a bona fide, certified Mommy who's actually going through toddlerhood and following the well-intentioned stranger around saying, "But..." and "What if...?" and "How come...?"

That's where this book comes in. As a Mommy on the brink of daily collapse and living through toddlerhood with each and every word typed (hold on a sec while I take a child off my leg), I'm not about to blow smoke your way and tell you that raising a toddler is easy and life should be full of cherry-scented farts. So here's the deal. I've actually teamed up with a nationally certified expert on behavior, and we've come up with a new and exciting application of a scientifically supported method of behavior analysis. You'll get all the innovative, professional inside secrets *and* the skinny on the realities involved in implementing the strategies. No more tossing how-to books across the room yelling, "Yeah, right! Hello? Real world? What about the days when one kid is throwing up all over the house, the other is squeezing toothpaste all over the curtains, and the dog has been outside barking at the fence for five straight hours? What the heck do I do then?"

Who Should Read This Book?

Parents, daycare workers, teachers, therapists, grandparents, aunts, uncles – anyone who deals with one, two, or three-year-olds can benefit from this book. But no two ways about it, main caregivers are the ones who will profit the most. The book is addressed to "Mommies", so forgive me if you're not a Mommy and feel a bit irked. Not my intention. Any "Mommy" role, as well as fathers, is enormously important!

If you've ever been motivated by a book on toddlers, yet quickly disappointed in the effort it takes and the lack of freaking reality the author's plan seems to possess, this book's for you, honey. Dr. Chandler is a highly sought after behavioral specialist (yeah, and *I* snagged her!) whose method for behavior analysis has been proven over and over again. And as a speech therapist and mother of three, my own background in behavior management allows me to understand the technical part, yet empathize with the very real emotions associated with toddler discipline: guilt, anger, fear, love – not to mention the physical and mental state of exhaustion we caregivers perpetually carry with us. Every bit affects our ability to raise happy children.

Toddlers sock you with a fat punch of reality, and all the 'specialists' with their stupid examples of perfect parenting are too damn depressing for a Mommy in the thick of it. The nonstop duties of feeding, diapering, playing, entertaining, refereeing, cleaning, and being nurse, lifeguard, and potty guidance counselor leave you too weary to muster up the energy to be a perfect Mommy. Where's the motivation to drag our sorry butts into the kitchen to fix our kids gourmet meals? We just love those fancy toddler cookbooks, but I'll be a flying monkey if they don't end up tossed into the pantry next to the stash of Cheetos® as we run to save a terrified child stuck behind the fridge.

If you're constantly being commanded by a very short person to do some oddball thing like help them remove the potty training seat from their neck or make a square block fit into a round hole, then you too are living the toddler-moment. You too are chasing roadrunners, dodging bites, fending off headaches, and loving the slobbery kisses in between. So when it comes to exhausting and feral behavior, feel certain I'm not about to let some 'expert' spout off confusing and unrealistic mumbo-jumbo. My Mommy duty is to be straight up with you about the rather stupefying aspects of raising a toddler. Are they supposed to flip out and act like fiends sometimes? Yep. Are we shirking our Mommy-duty if we occasionally (okay, frequently) feel like gulping down some Motrin and running straight to the nearest spa? Please. My friend, we've all been there – even if no one *else* is brave enough to admit it.

What's In it for Me?

What, specifically, will you gain by reading this book? Well honestly, if you just *read* it, you'll get *nada*. Sorry, dear. You can't make cookies without sticking them in the oven; they aren't going to bake themselves just because you mix up the dough and stare at it. However, if you change your thinking, implement the strategies, and stay committed to the process, you can change your life. Literally. You can turn around a world of tantrums, fighting, crying, whining, nagging, yelling, and misery.

You will gain time. You and your child will gain a mutual respect. You will gain a happy child, replacing the one you think is unhappy more than you'd like, or out of control more than you can handle. You will also gain relief, days of endless joy with your toddler (okay, maybe that's a stretch), sleep (now there's a miracle!), and an incredible knowledge base on what to do when things get rough. You will know *why* your little angel seems to be sprouting horns and exactly what you can do about it.

Most importantly, you will gain realistic options to eliminate problem behavior and make your child happy. That is key. Any old ape can dish out opinions, but if this person doesn't currently *have* a toddler, isn't (or has never been) the main caregiver of their kids, or isn't surrounded by their own little sweeties day in and day out...well. I'd caution you to be wary of any peachy advice, especially by someone lacking real-time emotional shock. When's the last time they dealt with *their* child fitfully rolling on the ground, screeching as if attacked by a swarm of invisible bees? Too long? Never? Mmm hmm. As I said, they can bite me.

The Toddler ABC Guide© or "TAG"

This book is based on our method for learning to understand your toddler and communicate effectively to increase desired behaviors. It's called "TAG" - the Toddler ABC Guide - and it will literally rock your world in a fabulous way. Here's the gist: First of all, think of a blank slate. In fact, don't think of your own child. Think of a stranger's child - someone in whom you have no expectations, no frustration, and no association of behavior nightmares. This helps you be objective. Now, here's the breakdown (And hey, don't get scared. I'm with you and we'll make it easy):

A stands for "Antecedent" = the event <u>before</u> the desired or undesired behavior.

B stands for "Behavior" = clearly defined in measurable and observable terms.

C stands for "Consequence" = what happens immediately after the behavior.

A = Antecedent

A is the event that happens right before the behavior. When you think of behavior, you've got two outcomes: desired or undesired. Good or bad. So you can look at the antecedent as the action or thing that 'causes' the good or bad behavior. Most often it's requests, actions, or commands from us such as "clean your room, turn that off, it's time to go, you can't have this," etc.

1) Identify A

What did you say? What did you do? What was your child doing? Figure out your set up. If the resulting behavior was good, set it up that way again. If the behavior was bad, change your set up. Do your best to prevent that behavior in the future.

2) Crystal clear direction and expectations

For the purpose of our guide, antecedents are used to provide preventive support (one of Dr. Chandler's mumbo-jumbo terms). Put simply, this means it's our job to make sure the child knows and understands every single word we say and give crystal clear directions, examples, and expectations to set up a successful outcome. A child cannot do what you want or ask if he doesn't understand what you want or ask. Many times a toddler will react to your request or command in whatever way they do understand or think you want.

Let's say you ask them to "be careful with the baby." What you really mean is, "stop pushing the baby." But how do they know that? You didn't actually say it! So they have to guess what 'be careful' means. And they guess you mean "don't run around the baby." So they don't run, but continue to push. You mistake it for defiance. The fact of the matter is, the request was not clear. Your child may have been trying to comply, but just didn't get what you wanted.

Confusing defiance with lack of understanding is a huge issue with toddler behavior and common mistake among caregivers. The next time you feel like barking, "Why won't you listen to me?!" think about it first. Consider that it's not a matter of listening, but comprehension. Ask yourself, are you using clear, concise, and specific words and requests they understand?

3) External Factors

Under **A** you also examine external factors such as lack of sleep, distractions, hunger/thirst, etc. Use this information to avoid conflict or misunderstandings. For example, Joe toddler is tired. You ask him to put on his pajamas and he continues to play, ignoring your request. Rather than get mad at him for not listening (again), you know he's just exhausted and needs physical help to get going with the request. The expectation doesn't change – he's still going to change clothes – but knowing that he's tired, you offer hands-on help. An outsider could immediately walk in and call this defiance, but you know why he's ignoring the request and you factor that in.

4) Set up for success

Provide physical and verbal prompts/cues (Chapter 3) to get the desired outcome with the least amount of resistance. This avoids the immediate conflict of yelling (or other unconstructive reactions) because you understand what works and how to direct behavior.

B = Behavior

1) Define It. **B** clearly defines the behavior and is more action-oriented. Look at this in terms that can be observed and measured. (Oh, this jargon is killing me. Truly.) You can't observe and measure aggression. But you can break it down into parts. How is he being aggressive? Throwing objects, screaming, hitting, biting? How many times a day, for how long, and how intense is it? Those are measurable. When you look at it this way, you get a better sense of improvement, or indication of the behavior getting worse. Being vague or abstract leaves you open to miscommunication and failure.

2) Give Specific Directions. Give your child specific directions so he understands how you want him to behave. He must understand exactly what you want. If you can't get your child to understand exactly how you want him to behave, then your approach won't work and the behavior will continue or become worse.

3) Use Clear Words. Avoid isolated abstract terms: 'be good', 'stop that', 'bad behavior', 'be nice'. Toddlers don't understand these things! Use age appropriate language, and pair the terms with specific actions. For example, "be good" can mean:

*nice walking	*soft touch
*say please	*say thank you
*use your words	*follow me
*walk beside me	*hands to yourself

"Be good" is too vague. Avoid fuzzy words! Be clear. Using specific words teaches your child exactly what behavior you want to see. Keep it positive. Think about what you WANT. Be specific, and stop telling your child what you *don't* want. That's a negative and clearly doesn't help the lovedoodle understand what you DO want!

Here are some examples:

Want	Don't Want
Quiet feet	No running!
Quiet mouth	Stop yelling!
Bottom on the chair	Quit wiggling!
Food goes in your mouth	Don't throw that!
Stay with Mommy	Don't you run from me!

Hands to yourself   Leave your brother alone!

See what I mean? Focus on what you WANT your child to do. When you always say, "stop it" or "no" or "cut it out", it doesn't tell them what you want to see instead. And they don't have a clue! You must tell them in words they understand.

Make sure the direction is age appropriate. A 15-month-old can't (on any consistent basis) 'touch softly'; it's not physically doable given their gross and fine motor skills. So asking her to 'touch the cat softly' will be a work in progress for a long while. If there's any chance the cat could scratch or bite if hurt, then it's probably better to teach your child the cat is a no-no – for a few months anyway. They do know and can physically refrain from touching something at 15 months, but allowing them to touch something only if it's done softly is just an agonizing battle.

C = Consequence

What happens after the behavior? (Remember, keep your slate blank.) The event should be clearly defined; exactly what did you do after the behavior? Here's an example:

A = Antecedent: You ask Junior to pick up his toys.

B = Behavior: Junior screams.

C = Consequence: You can:

1. Yell, spank, talk to him/give in (give the behavior attention),

Or

2. Ignore the screams and provide physical prompts to pick up the toys.

Consequences serve to either reinforce or punish the behavior. In the above example, the consequence of #1 reinforces the screaming, which is an undesired behavior. Bad! When you reinforce, toddlers continue the behavior because it works. The screaming is reinforced if you give it attention. And how do you give this negative/incorrect attention? By yelling, spanking, or getting all mushy or embarrassed because he's crying and you can't stand it. If you give in at all and don't make him clean up, you reinforce the screaming. It works, and by golly, he'll do it again.

So go the other route. The consequence of #2 punishes the behavior (even though you didn't react to it) and decreases the likelihood of recurrence because the child gets nothing out of it. No attention for the undesired behavior means it doesn't work for him. He still has to clean up the toys. This is a new way to look at what we parents think of "punishment". In this case, punishment is not aversive, harsh, demeaning, or disrespectful. It's simply a term to define a calm and peaceful reaction that decreases undesired behavior. Consider it written in stone:

Reinforcement (R) = Increases behavior

Punishment (P) = Decreases behavior

In the Toddler ABC Guide©, ***punishment is calm and peaceful***. If you can't stand the thought of calling it "punishment," call it whatever you want. "Deterrent" or "Prevent"…who really cares? Don't get caught up in semantics. It won't make a hill of beans of difference, people!

How to Read This Book

Obviously, Dr. Chandler and I advise reading this top to bottom because you'll get the 'why' behind development, tantrums, unwanted behavior, and strategies to resolve it. I can tell you all day long how to minimize bath time struggles, but if you don't understand *why* your little ducky throws a fit just as soon as you pull the drain – every single time – and you don't get *why* I tell you to do A, B, and C, then you can't very well apply the same strategies when the poop hits the fan because Jr. doesn't want to wear socks.

Big however: As a Mommy with absolutely no time, and understanding that everyone learns differently, this book is organized in such a way that you can read straight through and really study the program, or flip around to the parts you need during the one free minute you have each day (which would be…on the toilet?). The Toddler ABC Guide (TAG)© is used throughout, so at the very least, soak that in before heading off to page 80. The point of this book is to lay out the technical in a practical way, so at minimum, absorb the 'technical' TAG© into your noggin, and you should be good to start flipping to the practical stuff. Here's the breakdown on what's where:

Part I: Prevention: This section outlines our plan for preventing problem behavior, why terminology is so important, and basic foundations to skirt disaster before it pops up. Knowing the lingo (or some semblance thereof) is important, but sometimes intimidating. But this is me you're talking to, and I've made that dreaded technical stuff not-so-dreaded. Once you understand it, you'll realize how straight forward toddler discipline really is (although exhausting - I'm not a liar, here) and why it's been so easy to miss the forest for all the trees.

Part II: Application: This section outlines specific strategies to implement on a daily basis to increase cooperation and create an environment of trust, security, and control. We'll talk about how to change *your* actions in order to get the desired changes in your little love bug. Knowing how to manage behavior is like taking a happy pill. This section also details the importance of praise and patience, rewarding good behavior, sharing (ooooh, that *word!*), and how to deal with other children (and their Mommies, thank you very much) who are consistently aggressive, making you nuts.

Part III: Implementation: This section goes over specific toddler-related problems such as tantrums, biting, and bedtime struggles. To help with this, we provide a list of specific developmental stages of motor, language, and self-care skills as they relate to one, two, and three-year-olds. Remember, a child can't do what you ask if he isn't physically or cognitively able. This list gives you a heads up on what children can and can't do at specific ages.

The last chapter deals with how to be your best and give the best to your children. Thinking of yourself (what a novel concept!) and putting your own needs on a front burner is key to staying sane and putting your best discipline foot forward.

As a Mommy who understands the daily stresses and difficulties dealing with these little people, I know how hard it is to pick battles and do what the experts say. You love this child with every ounce of your being, but you're working...stressed...tired. I'm there. Right now, in fact! I've been going through toddlerhood for five straight years, and as I type this very sentence, my youngest just turned one, so there's another three ahead (dear God). The worry, guilt, and exhaustion never go away, but it does get better. But no matter what your toddler's age, you *can* learn to enjoy and cherish what little time they'll spend in this fabulous stage. (And okay, so it's not fabulous *now*, but maybe in five years you'll think so!)

Introduction Review: What Did We Learn?

Who should read this book and knowledge you'll gain.

TAG = Toddler ABC Guide and definitions of:

> **A = Antecedent**: event before the behavior (the trigger), preventive support, and external factors such as hunger, etc.

> **B = Behavior**: specifically defined. Give clear, positive instructions on what you WANT, not what you don't.

> **C = Consequence**: your reaction will (**R**) reinforce or (**P**) punish. Figure out why the child is acting out. Customize your response. Do NOT reinforce the behavior by giving in to the demand or giving him the attention he is shooting for.

How to turn negatives into positives: tell our kids what we WANT instead of what we **don't**.

Stop reinforcing negative behavior.

Start reinforcing what you WANT to see.

Punish negative behavior – remember, (**P**) is not harsh!

Tell and Show your child exactly what you want to see and how you want them to act – otherwise, they won't know!

Avoid fuzzy words (stop that, no, cut it out, be nice, be good, that's bad). Spell out what you want, keep it positive, and be specific!

 Break down of part I (Prevention), II (Application), and III (Implementation).

Chapter One: Why Do They Act Like That?

Being a frank and simple gal, I'm going to give it to you straight: As the Mommy of three, I have no time to pee. If I offend, get over it, because there's also no time to eat, think, or breathe, so there's no time left to soften the blow. Sure, given the fact that I'm writing a book on toddler discipline, you would think I could control my kids long enough to carve out fifteen whole seconds and make a dash to the "little room" to relieve my bursting bladder. Not so.

The awful truth is that there really are days when there's no time. Please, you know what I mean. Our own bodily demands get pushed right off the priority list. We're too busy meeting all the catastrophic needs of the tiny people dashing through the house. Toddler needs being an endless abyss, it means a zenith eventually slams us in the bladder, forcing a decision. And what do we Mommies do? Leave our three-year-old at the dinner table to finger-paint with the peas she's mashed? Let our one-year-old bawl her eyes out (over who knows what) in the middle of the living room floor? Or just leave it all to fate and wet ourselves because we can't seem to tear away from our demanding little brood?

The Five Basics Are Essential!

Go ahead and be adult. Tee-tee in that big girl potty. While you're butt is planted (and okay, you're rushed and it's only 4 seconds), think about the foundation to establish so these wrenching decisions on whether to pee or not to pee are minimized. Here it is, plain and simple: All children need **The Five Basics**: Structure, Communication, Limits, Consistency, and Guidance.

1. Structure is a schedule or predictable routine. Most kids thrive on knowing what will come next and what to expect. Structure gives toddlers security. When you do the same things every day, at the same time, they feel a sense of order and control. Think about the routine at preschool: same activities, same time, every day. The kids know what to expect, and they cooperate. You cannot give them a nap at 1 p.m. one day, then 3 p.m. the next, then no nap at all the day after that. You must have structure. I know life gets in the way sometimes, but you have to try your best.

If you don't give your child a consistent routine, don't expect them to act well behaved. Some kids are more agreeable than others, but for the love of Pete, don't drag them all over creation, then get confused and angry when they act like a tyrant. RESPECT a routine.

2. Communication: Mind blowing important! You have to communicate effectively to your toddler using words they understand, and your toddler must be able to communicate needs to you (and you must listen!) Without communication, you're hosed. Just do something –anything–to get a mode of communication going. Toddlers MUST be able to communicate or they'll go into overload and throw a holy fit.

3. Limits are restricted choices and boundaries (to spoil or not to spoil...that is the question, Shakespeare). By giving toddlers limited choices, you're still giving them the freedom to make decisions, but sparing the overload of having too much to choose from. All children need limits to feel secure, in control, and safe.

4. Consistency builds trust and shapes behavior by continually letting toddlers know what's acceptable and not. When children trust you, they do what's asked, because they know consequences are consistent. When you're not consistent, you just confuse the poor baby. They don't know what you want or how to act.

5. Guidance provides alternatives to undesirable behavior. Listen to me here!! Rather than say, "No!" all the time, tell kids what they CAN do. Giving proper guidance teaches kids how to approach getting what they want in a positive way, which eliminates the cycle of negative attention. Oooooh, we Mommies give too much negative attention!

A Sign of Peace for Honest Mommies: I used to be one of those people who'd see a screaming toddler in a department store and snottily hiss, "*My* children will never act like *that!*" Ten years and two kids later, guess who's vigorously juggling baby bottles, boxed juice, and tearing open packages of peanut butter crackers, all in the attempt to console her two irrationally hungry, cranky, and LOUD children? Oh, the pain of it all. Someone give me an aspirin! Boxed fruit drinks do nothing but shoot liquid sugar out of the straw and caramelize our kids, thus cranking up the crying. Dish me up a cup of stupid for passing the damn things out. Like I don't have enough ear-splitting racket to contend with.

The maddening commotion made me stop short, sucking in a breath of horror-struck realization. And so came the epiphany, right there on aisle five of the local grocery store. I had been thrust into the group of harried Mommies and bratty kids that other people either glare at or sympathize with. Bewildering!

So when I share these moments of madness (and historically pathetic parenting skills), it's only as a sign of peace; a gesture of sympathy to all caregivers of toddlers. We put on a good front, but deep down we just want to know if there are others out there, sharing our frustration and simultaneous love and commitment to our babies. As caregivers of toddlers, we're all the same. Our hearts have been stolen and we're helplessly devoted. (And tired. Yes, very tired!)

We Mommies are in this together, and if you think you've got it bad because you don't have time to shower, take my admission of no time to eat, pee, or breathe, and run with it. You are not alone in this toddler race, so exhale a deep sigh of relief, baby. The rest of us are out there huffing and puffing just like you. As Mommies, we're united and share the most difficult of jobs. We must not break down when our babies suffer from colic. We must not faint when our toddler throws up all over Santa Claus (*Great balls of fire!*). We must band together to keep our sanity! Just because I've written a book on toddler discipline doesn't mean I'm perfect and my children don't have a meltdown every time they drop their beloved cookies. If they acted ideal, what kind of inspiration would that be?

Conceding to having strong opinions on discipline is easy. But I'm also not arrogant enough to believe it's all so cut and dried. I have great plans for "what to do if," but in reality, I don't always have the answers. Nobody does. As a matter of fact, as I write this very sentence, my daughter is trying to tear her crib apart in a raging, violent, screaming fit after being banished to her room. The offense? God, I've already forgotten. I'm too caught up in the shrieks – can't even think straight and remember. And as a thoroughly confused Mommy, I can only sit here and debate whether to laugh, cry, leave her alone, hug her, or call up a girlfriend and have my own hysterical fit. So, ha! How's that for being an expert?!

The Recipe

When it comes to discipline, you will get out what you put in. Your toddler is a direct reflection of what you give him or her. The problem is, *how* and *what* you give is as important as *how much* you give. It's like a good recipe. Giving all you've got is not the key. You can put everything in your pantry into a boiling pot and it'll come out a stinky mess. *What* you put in and *how* you do it makes all the difference. For a good stew, you need vegetables, not fruit. And the vegetables need to be cut up. You can't put whole carrots and celery into the pot and expect it to fit, much less soak up the good juices.

16

It's the same with your toddler. You have to figure out his recipe. He's individual and unique, having his own set of rules for what will work. To figure out what ingredients make him tick, you need to look at what he's telling you. If you don't look at the behavior and what it conveys, you're continuing to put fruit in your stew. It just won't work and will never come out as you expect.

Whenever you feel like pulling out every strand of your expensively colored hair, stop and reset. Your child is trying to tell you something. Stop and listen. Example: Little Collin howls in protest when refused ten more Teddy Trooper accessories. Instead of getting a headache just thinking about the battle ahead (which, by the way, ends in your darling getting what he wants), step back and look at what the behavior conveys. Take the time to assess the reason behind the tantrum. What does he want? Why does he use that method? Are you reinforcing the behavior? Do you always give in? Put the effort into changing *your* approach so you get the desired change in *him*.

You will only get out what you put in. Girly, if you don't change your attitude and approach, there is no way on Earth your child will change what's working so favorably. Put simply, if you always do what you've always done, you'll always get the same results.

Discipline Must Be Delicate, Firm, and Consistent

Talk may be tough at times, but my belief is resolute: **when it comes to discipline, you must be delicate and consistent**. In my work as a speech therapist and Mommy, the observation is always the same - being delicate and consistent works. Even if the kid is acting so horrible that you feel like selling her to the highest bidder, there's no benefit to being anything other than calm and kind. Yes, you need to be firm, but that doesn't equal being mean or using any form of verbal abuse or physical retribution such as swatting, slapping, or spanking. Once in a *great* while a small pop on the hiney might snap a kid out of hysteria,

17

but truly, it's not often. It really depends on personality and circumstance. Personally, I'd avoid it. There are better ways.

Firm kindness is easy as long as you're consistent with your follow through and throw the guilt monster out the window. And I do mean *throw it out!* Realistically, no, we won't always be unswerving, delicate, and calm every minute of the day. We've all got hot buttons. The witching hours between dinner and bedtime are just crap. Good gravy, the fatigue! (The only thing I generally care about is a bed, and not in a sexy way, little girlfriend!) But even when tired, stressed, sick, or we just need a break, effective discipline depends on our attitude and interpretation of the problem. We need to be objective, stay firm, and keep our emotions in check if at all possible. Maintaining your cool is no walk in the park. When your toddler is about thirty seconds from choking the life out of a younger sibling, we're spitting flames. But tempering that fury is important.

Meeting Needs to Make Kids Happy

Discipline, in a true sense, is about giving kids what they need to make them happy. You might have a hotheaded old uncle who suggests the kid "needs" a good whack on the fanny, but Uncle Crankpot is probably way off base. To meet the needs of children, it's essential to look at the "why" behind undesired behaviors. Reading and meeting needs is proactive, and gets your child's recipe right. It works. Yelling, threatening, arguing, or otherwise reinforcing the behavior does not. When needs are met, your child is secure and happy and will have no reason to drop to the ground acting like a screaming banshee twelve times a day.

Here's another example of TAG in action:

Set up: You're getting ready to step into the shower and your toddler brings you a book to read.

A = You say, "I can't read to you now; I have to take a shower."

B = Child falls to the floor and starts crying

C = You can:

> **P** = Ignore the behavior and get into the shower

> Or

> **R** = say, "Oh, okay, I'll read just one book."

What's the 'need' here? Easy. It's guidance. She needs guidance on how to act appropriately to get what she wants. By choosing **P** (= punish) you eliminate the behavior because it won't work for the child. In contrast, **R** (= reinforce) only reinforces the idea that falling to the floor and crying achieves her goal. She'll do it again because it works. So not only do you delay your shower by sitting down naked and smelly to read to your child, you've just given her very clear instructions that it's perfectly okay to cry and throw a fit to get what she wants. This doesn't meet her need, my dear!

Now for a reality check. As the Mommy of a toddler, you're doomed to suffer through an occasional poltergeist tantrum – not matter what you do. Toddlers will be toddlers and go ballistic sometimes. They're untamed, completely void of emotional restraint, and often lack the simple language to express frustration and anger. It takes time for them to learn how to communicate effectively *and* realize they aren't the center of the universe. That's okay. One or two monthly episodes of foaming at the mouth and rolling on the floor in a raging fit wouldn't even phase me, much less have me worried about neglecting needs.

However, daily kicking, screaming, hitting, beating up siblings, throwing food, and giving you migraines...THAT is not okay. And it means _you_ are the one that needs to change. This doesn't mean you blame yourself when your children act out, but you must accept a better way to discipline.

When children act out, it should tell you they're not happy and lacking something that's your responsibility to give. Now, when referring to "acting out", we're talking *aggressive* behavior. The nutso stuff. You can't expect your kids to neatly clean their plate, keep peanut butter out of their ears and hair, pick up all their toys, not eat books, stay out of the cat food, and act like perfect little angels. If you don't let them discover what happens when they dump grape juice on their head (and by the way, *why* are you giving them dark purple sure-to-stain juice?) or let them express a little anger, it can hold back their cognitive, physical, and emotional development.

Defining 'Needs': Why Children Act Out

Here are some basic needs kids have and reasons for acting out:

1. They want attention OR

2. Want to be left alone.

3. They are unable to communicate what they want (verbal or gestures).

4. They want a particular object, action, person, or activity.

5. They *don't* want a particular object, action, person, or activity.

6. They are tired, hungry or overstimulated.

7. To gain sensory stimulation (a particular action feels good – i.e. biting).

8. Big change in life (new house, new baby, family death, no bottle, etc.).

9. They feel insecure or out of control (emotional needs).

10. They are uncomfortable, sick, or hurting.

11. They have difficulty with transitions from one activity to the next.

Once you figure out why a behavior is present, make the effort to change your approach to the problem. Really think about what your toddler is trying to express. Other than the above examples, it will likely be one of **The Five Basics** of **structure, communication, limits, consistency, or guidance**. Emotional needs must also be met. Children need to feel loved and cared for. You must give them your time and attention!

Translate Please! Looking at the list above, let's translate into daily wants/needs.

1. Attention – the #1 biggie: Listen up! Toddlers MUST feel loved! They have to know you're paying attention and care. We do absolutely no good for a child when we sit them in front of a T.V. so they'll leave us alone. Pay attention to them. Play with them. Talk to them. Give hugs and kisses. Forget about "stuff" or buying them gifts. They could care less. They want your eye contact, love, time, and genuine affection. Give it to them.

2. Wants to be Left Alone: Now, on the other side, hello! Sometimes they want to be left alone. The poor kid could be desperate for slumber, but nooooo! We still feel the need to pass Jr. around the family reunion like he's a pet kitten. Or, he's playing quite nicely with a stuffed dog, yet we keep shoving a new toy truck in his face – because by golly, Grandma just bought it! She'll be crushed if he doesn't like it. Heavens alive, girlfriend, cut that out! Leave him alone!

3. Communication: Toddlers need to share what they're thinking. They have to be able to communicate pain (emotional and physical), hunger, sadness, questions, joys, etc. This doesn't have to be with words. They communicate with facial expressions, pointing, grunts, vocalizations, simple eye contact, and behavior. They communicate what they want with their actions.

4. Want Object/Action/Person/Activity: They do this daily and nonstop. And again, if they cannot communicate these wants, you're up a creek.

5. Don't Want Object/Action/Person/Activity: They'll express this quite obviously by turning away, swatting the object away, crying, pitching a fit, or ignoring. LISTEN to them. Do not keep shoving a bottle, binky, or sandwich in their mouth if they clearly don't want it!

6. Tired, Hungry, Over-stimulated: Toddlers are cranky when tired or hungry. So keep a ROUTINE of meals, snacks, and sleep. Same time, everyday! And as far as stimulation...honey, we need a heart to heart between us gals. Toddlers cannot handle malls, state fairs, concerts, trips out of town, weddings, etc. – at least not on a consistent basis. It's no big deal to adults, but to toddlers, it's way too much. People talking, loud music, visual bombardment, a wrecked routine (most of the time we're skipping a nap to attend these functions)...it's simply overwhelming to little brains.

Give the kid a break!! Keep a schedule, and do not drag the poor child all over creation. They'll act like a monkey and you'll wonder why. <u>Keep stimulation (visual and verbal) to a minimum at all times!!!</u> That means no loud T.V., blaring music, motorcycles, tons of kids, parties, dogs barking, family fights, and whatever else.

7. Sensory Stimulation: Toddlers get a sense of texture by biting and chewing. It's actually part of their brain development. So it's not always vicious when they bite your arm – they just like the squishy aspect!

8. Big Changes in Life: Consistency - remember that one? Change rocks their world. They like **simple and same**. Routine, routine, routine! Changes, especially big ones, make them feel very insecure.

9. Insecure/Out of Control (Emotional Needs): Emotional needs are huge!! Children need to feel loved and cared for. You must give them your time and attention. They get a sense of security with structure, routine, limits, and consistency. The world is too big to process, so narrow it down for them. Give them security.

10. Uncomfortable, Sick, Hurting: You know this one. Don't feel good = cranky. Sometimes, though, we don't know pain is the problem. Teeth don't always advertise, and stomach viruses sneak up on you. Pay attention and make sure they're not in physical pain.

11. Transitions: Another biggie. Some kids do better than others, but for the most part, it's difficult to leave one activity for another unless they're ready. More on this later...

Let's look at another example: Little Emma has a melt down every time you ask her to get out of the bathtub. Think about what the behavior tells you. Is bath time consistent every night? If not, she may be feeling insecure and needs more consistency. Or, could it be a problem transitioning from one task to another (playing in the tub to getting dressed)? If that's the case, she needs more guidance on transitions. Could it be she's exceedingly tired? Or wants to continue playing in the tub and you generally give in when the howling starts? Maybe she's asking for firm limits; bath is over and it's time for bed. Limits are especially tough for us wimpy parents to enforce. It's easy to think restricting playtime and choices or saying "no" to requests will make us the bad guy. The opposite is true. Kids feel very secure when their boundaries are clear and they're not forced to make constant mind-boggling decisions.

Look for the red flags and flares. It's your toddler's attempt at communication. Needs are not being met. Sometimes we can figure out what they want, and sometimes we can't. But don't get caught up in quick reactions to the behavior. Step back and give yourself a few seconds to assess the real problem. Once you figure it out, FIX IT. Do your part and change the way you react to the behavior. **If what you're doing isn't working, then holy cow, CHANGE it!**

The Learning Curve

As much as I preach about meeting needs and reading the clues kids give, any conscious Mommy would assume I've got this detective business down pat. Not so. It's a continual learning process. Each day brings new challenges and insights. For example, one day Poppy (my oldest daughter) wanted to get on the computer to play a game, and I wanted to take a shower. I told her several times, "It's not time to play on the computer. Please come with Mommy and let's take a shower." Wanting no part of my cleaning ritual, she immediately went limp and started howling. Five minutes of time-out had her sniffling, but recovered and in control. Later in the day, thinking about what went wrong, it dawned on me that we didn't actually *have* a specific time of day designated to let her play on the computer. So when I told her it wasn't time to play, she didn't have a frame of reference as to when it *was* time. Prior to this incident, I'd been randomly letting her work on the computer whenever she wanted to.

My daughter was simply going along with what I had established as a pattern and was upset because I said no. Resolving the matter was as easy as setting up two specific times during the day when she could play her computer games. The increase in cooperation was immediate. I set up the times, repeated the new rule every time she asked to play her games, and consistently let her play during the designated periods. If it wasn't possible for her to play during her designated time, I promised she could get on the computer after we completed the conflicting task. Come hell or high water, I kept that promise. All it takes is stepping back and looking at a situation, then changing *your* approach to produce a positive outcome.

Stop Being Such a TOOT!!! At the risk of sounding harsh, I'll make this point loud and clear because it's too important to miss. *If your child consistently acts like a toot, it means the negative behavior is consistently being rewarded.* Oh yes, baby doll. You are the one responsible. As a consequence to the undesired behavior, time and again you're choosing **R** in the Toddler ABC Guide and **reinforcing** the unwanted behavior.

If little Emily unfailingly gets a piece of candy to quiet her down every time she howls in church or when you're on the phone, you're rewarding the behavior and teaching her that she gets what she wants when she howls. If Emily gets your undivided (albeit angry) attention when she throws a tantrum, then she's being rewarded with your presence. When fits of defiance are the only way she'll get your interest, that's what she'll do. Angry Mommy attention is better than no Mommy attention.

Analyze and Customize with TAG

You have to analyze *"WHY"* your toddler is acting unfavorably and customize the consequence. Here's an example: You unfailingly give a time-out for any and all hitting, yet the time-out only works sporadically. Confusing? Not really. Look at the motivating factors. If your child stops hitting when you give a time-out, you're pinning the tail on the donkey because you've tuned into what your child wants and you deny it. The time-out acts as a true deterrent (**P**) because it encourages cooperation and stops the behavior. However, if the hitting continues, your consequence of a time-out may not deny your child what he wants, and could actually be reinforcing the hitting. Even though the behavior (hitting) is the same, the time-out will fail if your child's motivating factors have changed.

Let's do a TAG:

Scenario #1

>A = Little Tony wants Homer's toy car

>B = Tony hits Homer and takes the car

>C = You can:

>>P = Take the car and put Tony in time-out

>>Or

>>R = scold Tony for hitting, then let him continue playing

Now let's change the motivating factors:

Scenario #2

>A = You say to Tony, "It's time to go home."

>B = Tony cries and hits you twice

>C = You can:

>>P = Take his arm and say, "No hitting," then leave; take Tony home as you said

>>Or

>>R = Stay at Homer's house; put Tony in time-out

Do you see how the consequence of time-out will work in scenario #1 and not in #2? In Scenario #2, putting Tony in time-out at Homer's house achieves Tony's goal. He gets to stay. Chances are, you'll start yammering with Homer's mom and bingo! He's gotten another thirty minutes of play out of you.

Looking at the 'why' behind behavior tells you how to proceed with your punishment (**P**) and stop reinforcing the unwanted behavior. Sometimes putting your boxing champ in a time-out does not solve the entire problem and pins the tail on the donkey's ear. If little Tony is hitting out of frustration rather than attention, separation is still appropriate, but it's not the entire answer to the problem.

He may also have a *NEED* that should be addressed. It's possible he needs more modeling and guidance on how to act appropriately in that particular situation in addition to a short time-out to diffuse the anger and aggravation. Sticking him in a time-out and expecting that alone to nix the problem is like cooking only one side of a pancake and expecting it to taste good.

More examples:

Dean: My friend Jennifer gave me a great example with her son Dean. At daycare, he consistently acted up during snack time. The consequence – taking away his snack – only worked half the time. He would always stand or dance on his chair and be uncooperative when his caregivers attempted to get him seated for snack. When they took the snack away, sometimes he'd cooperate and sit down, and sometimes he wouldn't.

- If Dean is actually hungry, taking the snack away is a good behavioral deterrent. He straightens up so he can eat.

- If he's not hungry, taking away the snack makes no difference - he could care less!

So the consequence of taking away the snack doesn't always work even though the behavior is the same. Denying him food until he straightens up will only be successful if he's hungry.

If his caregivers want him to stop acting inappropriately when he's not hungry, they need to look at why he's standing on the chair. If attention is the goal, they need to put him in a time-out, giving him absolutely no attention. Then his caregivers need to work with him on a more appropriate way of getting what he wants, such as verbally asking someone to read a story or play with him.

Greg: Greg acted completely out of character at preschool and got into trouble by refusing to sit in the song circle and sing, "Frosty the Snowman." Very loudly demonstrating the words to *other* songs, he was getting up, dancing around, and would not cooperate with his teacher's requests to stop. Feeling like she had no other option, his teacher put him in a time-out. Upon hearing this at the end of the day, his mom took him aside and said, "Greg, you look upset. What's wrong honey?" He sadly replied, "Mom, I can't remember the words to Frosty the Snowman."

Haley: Dr. Chandler had another heart-wrenching story about the need to analyze and customize. She'd been working with a child who just wasn't responding to any technique she tried. Despite several different approaches, Haley wasn't making a shred of progress. Dr. Chandler decided to step back and look at the big picture. She knew she wasn't approaching the situation correctly because Haley wasn't reacting positively to any method she attempted. She determined further testing was needed, and it turned out Haley had a massive ear infection and hearing loss. It was no wonder she wasn't cooperating - she couldn't hear a word Dr. Chandler said! She covered up any symptoms of ear pain, so her caregiver didn't even realize the infection existed, let alone how much damage it caused. Haley was treated, fitted for hearing aids, and made immediate progress with Dr. Chandler's techniques.

Take the time to think about why your child is acting out. Customize each response. Think before you react and listen to what your child is communicating.

Bribes, Rewards, Reinforcers, and Consequences

So I call Dr. Chandler all the time. Yep. My personal, on-call therapist (yipee!) always there for me as soon as my toddlers hit the floor in a heaping tantrum. (By the way, did I mention this wonderful resource happens to be my very generous older sissy? Ha!) In the noble attempt to educate me, and rattling off a bunch of headache-yielding technical gibberish, my sister Rita (excuse me, *Doctor* Chandler) will generally have me snapping, "Slow down and speak English!" You know girlfriend, your brain gets crispy fried having so many kids. It really does freaking hurt to concentrate so hard. To that she always replied, "But Michelle, you need to understand the difference between blah-blah-blah and yak-yak-yak." (Okay. Are you weeping with me yet, people?) Pul-*eze*, give me the bottom line on what to do! Now! Of course she'd just singsong reply, "If you knew the difference, you could figure it ooout!"

Uh! Sweet mother of mercy! But all right, maybe she has a valid point. (And really, she *is* nice enough to lend me her services for free.) To approach discipline with our best foot forward, we need to have our little duckies in a row. So let's define **bribe** and **reward,** and tie it in with **consequence** and **reinforcer.** Most everyone knows how to reinforce *good* behavior, but we're darn clueless when reinforcing the unwanted stuff as well. Time to stop! Now, some of the terminology

29

can get a bit confusing, so stick with me. We'll interpret my sister's technical jargon into Mommy-ese and get groovin', okey dokey?

Bribes: When you bribe, you reinforce undesirable behavior. Example: Sweet pea howls for candy in the grocery store, and you pop a piece in her mouth to keep her quiet and refrain from embarrassing you. That's a bribe. You're bribing her to keep quiet, and reinforcing the behavior. This action clearly tells your child that she gets her way when she howls, which is an undesirable behavior.

Rewards: To promote good behavior, try something else; set up a reward system. Have it in place ahead of time. Before you step foot in the store, inform your little darling that if she cooperates by doing x, y, and z (remember, they need specific behaviors you <u>want</u> to see: "use a quiet voice, stay close to Mommy, walk slowly", etc.), she may get a reward when you get back home. It sounds like a bribe, but actually promotes and **rewards** good behavior. Bribes promote and reward *undesirable* behavior.

A good way to distinguish whether or not you're bribing is to look at <u>when</u> and <u>what</u> you offer as a peace saver. A bribe offers exactly what your little dictator demands *after* the howling and tantrums start. This "rewards" negative behavior. Bad! Conversely, a GOOD reward gives your child an incentive to cooperate *before* any yells fire up. This promotes desired behavior.

To take the reward route:

- Clearly state the expectations before hand, concentrating on what you want to see.

- The reward must be something your child desires. The more he wants it, the more powerful it is for you.

- Before you hit the store, let Jr. know that we use a quiet mouth while inside. If he cooperates, he will get "X".

- Do NOT tell him things like "no yelling", "don't be loud", "no running", "don't talk like that", or "stop arguing." First of all, those are things you *don't* want. Second, they are not specific. "Quiet mouth, slow feet, nice words" – that's what you want. It specifically states the behavior you want to see in terms your child can understand.

If you get in trouble and find yourself offering a bribe, turn it around.

1. Tell Jr. he can have 'Y' when he has 'a quiet mouth'. Do NOT say, "when you stop crying", "when you hush up", or "when you don't do that."

2. Do not offer the original "want" that started the crying. We do NOT reward throwing fits!

If he starts howling because he wants chips, offer some raisins or a bite of bagel instead. I know this sounds lame, but if it's in a cool package, he won't care. This is okay because it gets you out of the technicality of a bribe. Just don't make it your norm or you'll teach Jr. that crying still ultimately earns him a reward.

When your child cooperates, give the reward you promised. As far as what to give, the sky's the limit. Here are some examples of rewards. Pick a category in which your child responds best.

1. Sensory: brush hair, play makeup, scratch back, pleasant sounds, smells, or food

2. Tangible: stickers, books, non-food

3. Privilege: T.V. for 30 minutes (when otherwise off limits)

4. Generalized: Token system; money, marbles in a jar

5. Social: get to play at a friend's house or invite a friend over to make cookies

You can set up a chart of stickers, marbles in a jar, or whatever your little precious desires. The theory behind the sticker and jar (token) system is this: each time your toddler cooperates with your requests, they get one sticker on their chart or one marble in a jar. When the chart or jar is full, your child gets some big prize such as a trip to the toy store, zoo, or favorite hamburger joint. The only down side is that you have to be consistent, and even then, the novelty could wear off and the kid could end up being about as motivated for the reward as you are for a colonoscopy. To avoid this, make the ultimate reward quick at first. Three marbles or stickers and they get a prize. Then start making them accumulate more tokens before cashing in for a reward.

When a chart or jar of anything other than acetaminophen sounds like too much trouble, promise an extra book and cuddle (tangible and sensory), a movie with your undivided attention (privilege and social), or whatever motivates. This technique really works. Kids get very excited at the promise of, say, popcorn and a favorite movie if they're cooperative in the store. (This does, of course, go under the assumption they're not in front of the darn tube all day anyway. That's a "bad", my friend!) While you shop, keep her motivated with reminders of the reward and praise for good behavior.

If by chance, your dumpling decides to ignore your generous offer and howl because it's always worked before, DO NOT give in. You can pack up and leave right away, or take her outside, let her finish the tantrum, then go back in and continue your shopping. Whatever happens, *do not* give her the piece of candy or whatever started the howling. Be brave and consistent. Hold your ground. You will have to deal with this at some point or another, and if you give in, you've lost the battle. DO NOT WIMP OUT!

As a lovely coincidence and example, one of my own children once threw a MONSTROUS fit, which I unknowingly set up. Poppy asked to ride in a special cart at the grocery store. I said, "Sure!" She was jazzed and happy until I realized I couldn't get her in it – I had two smaller kids with me and they couldn't walk. They had to go in the cart, and she had to toddle along behind. Trying to appease her was futile; she wanted to ride in the car-cart like I promised. Holy Moly Gazoly, I caught hell. Screaming, screeching, scratching, kicking, knocking things over kind-of-hell. I'm frankly surprised a bomb squad wasn't called in, so awful was the entire scene.

Two lessons here:

1. I crushed her expectations. This could've been avoided had I thought ahead. Instead, I told her one thing, got her excited, then changed plans. We can't do that, girlfriend.

2. Even though it was my screw-up, I held my ground and didn't give her what she wanted. By the end of the horrendous ordeal, she was exhausted, I was thoroughly embarrassed and scarred for life, but she was cooperative.

The less experience your toddler has with yelling to get what she wants, the less time it'll take her to realize you mean business. If the behavior is chronic, it'll take more effort and endurance on your part. Stick to your guns and don't give in to the tantrums and demands. Remember girl, I feel your pain. If I can do it, you can do it.

Don't worry if the behavior gets worse before it gets better. In fact, expect it if your child is used to getting her way. When you suddenly change the rules, your determined toddler will persuade you to admit defeat by pumping up the volume and getting in a few more karate chops. If it has always worked before, she'll have no reason to believe cranking it up a notch won't work now. It may take some time, but once she realizes you aren't kidding, life will be a whole lot easier.

Consequence: As we learned in TAG, a consequence is the event that happens after a behavior. It can be yelling, a time-out, loss of a privilege, or as simple as the reaction of a caregiver. Consequences serve to either reinforce (R) or punish (P) behavior. For example, if little Jessica spits, her Mommy can react in any number of ways. Mommy just has to look at whether or not her response works in stopping the behavior. Then she can decide if the consequence is a reinforcer or a punishment.

When the response works and the spitting stops, the consequence is **P**. If the spitting does *not* stop, the consequence is **R**. If Jessica's goal in spitting is simply to get Mommy's attention, then any attention is **R**. In order to curb the behavior, Mommy would do well to just ignore the spitting. But, if Jessica spits only because she saw another child do it, Mommy's negative reaction (consequence), is not Jessica's goal. Here, Mommy could deter the behavior by simply telling Jessica, "We do not spit."

Review of Reinforcers:

Remember: If an undesired behavior increases or remains consistent, your reaction is a reinforcer (**R**).

Here's another example:

> **A** = child is eating lunch in highchair
>
> **B** = child stands up in highchair
>
> **C** = you can:
>
>> **P** = make her sit back down
>>
>> **R** = yell at her to sit down

By yelling or giving attention to the behavior, you are reinforcing. Little Joanna toddler will quickly demise how cool it is to get you all keyed up, and continue to stand for attention. Communication could be another motivator here. Standing in the chair could be her signal that she's finished. Instead of yelling and reinforcing, simply make her sit back down. Instruct her how to use gestures or words to tell you she's finished.

Reinforcing negative behavior is tough to avoid. There is something called *differential reinforcement*, and it's extremely important because we can unknowingly reinforce an undesired behavior when we think we're actually teaching a positive. Example: A child screams to get a cookie and you want to teach him how to ask appropriately. You instruct him to say 'cookie' (or show you a picture of a cookie), and he gets the cookie when he acts out the desired behavior.

Here's the clincher: Even if he shows you the picture just as you instructed, he has to <u>stop yelling</u> before you give him the cookie. Otherwise, you're reinforcing a *paired unwanted behavior* – the screaming. Technically, you have to wait until he stops screaming AND performs the desired/appropriate request before he gets the cookie. I know, it seems terribly unfair! The best thing to do is wait for the moment he catches his breath. If he stops screaming long enough to scratch his nose, as long as he's doing some part of the desired behavior, give him that cookie!

Chapter One Review: What Did We Learn?

The Five Basics to promote positive behavior:

1. Structure

2. Communication

3. Limits

4. Consistency

5. Guidance

How to figure out your child's recipe.

Discipline must be delicate, firm, and consistent.

How to assess Needs.

11 basic Needs and why toddlers act out.

How to customize our responses and stop reinforcing negative behavior.

Bribes, rewards, reinforcers, and consequences.

Five examples of rewards.

The no-no's of differential reinforcement.

Chapter Two: Stop Being a Ninny!

I have this theory that everything revolves around the behavior of your children. Think about it. Say your day starts off okay. Breakfast, dishes, laundry... you're rockin' and getting it done. Then, the gods of ill fortune conspiring against you, things go downhill. You walk into the living room to discover that the cat, who wasn't supposed to be inside in the first place, has thrown up all over the cream colored carpet. Your curious toddler is about two inches from maximum inspection. Luckily your screams of "NOOOO!" divert the little one's attention and you get to the scene of the crime before those chubby fingers squish the goo, giving him the bright idea to feed it to baby sister.

No sooner do you get the mess cleaned up then you're off to the next spill zone. You find your future artist making a magnificent masterpiece on your white bathroom cabinets with your favorite magenta lipstick and forty-dollars-a-bottle liquid foundation. Eight hours later, you still haven't showered, you're out of milk, the baby's got an ugly rash, and your toddler's normal two-hour nap was shortened by half after waking up with a poopy diaper. Heaven forbid he actually go back to sleep after you change him. Noooo, no. No can do.

By six p.m., Junior's wailing his head off, fighting the fourth time-out of the day for attempting to flush the very-much-alive-goldfish down the toilet. Now, one scenario is that you're all alone. Your spouse could be working, traveling, golfing, or off with his new wife and new freaking kids. The other scenario is that he IS home but uninterested, or he's about to *arrive* home and get a wild-eyed, over-tired, and downright frightening stare-of-a-greeting. Do you think he'll sympathetically rush to your side, offer an immediate comforting hug and ask you to tell him all about it? Ha! Not in this lifetime. He's got his own problems, and besides – who the hell wants to walk home to that?! So it's bad-mood-ville for everyone involved. I'm telling you, the kids rule the roost when it comes to setting the mood for the evening, morning, and whole course of the day.

You're Not the Boss of Me!

So, do we just throw in the towel and accept our destiny? Do we let our kids determine the mood for the day until they decide to move out and (please God) go to college? Do we hold our collective breath and hope to heaven our kids don't wear us flat by pouring bleach all over the couch and kick us every time we're in range? Good gracious, NO!

Okay Mommy, brace yourself because this is where I get callous and tell it like it is. Here's the bottom line:

YOU ARE THE BOSS!

Yep, that's it in a nutshell. You alone have the power to turn undesired behavior around. The discipline ball is in your court. You are the one who sets the stage for the entire day, ensuring your kids are happy, in control, and pleasant to be around. When the mood heads down the tubes, it's your job to assess what to do differently.

Ever hear a parent say, "Jr. just wouldn't let me take a shower or eat this morning"? Well, forget that. Wimp! Kids don't "let" you do (or not do) anything. *We* let our kids. We let them order us around, make us feel guilty, and tell us when we can bathe. This is not okay! For you rather lenient Mommies, this means (I will be very politically incorrect and give it to you straight) *stop being a pansy!* Get tough and consistent!

Now wait a second! Don't light this book on fire just yet. I'm not here to be judgmental of your parenting skills. Spineless parental inaction affects us all – even me. This does NOT mean you have to become some heavy-handed monster. Rather, you must simply take the initiative, be firm, and turn things around. Not so easy for some of us.

Isn't it second nature to look into the doey eyes of our greatest accomplishment on Earth and excuse every tiny thing that secretly drives us to exhaustion? How can we Mommies not give in when our little patootie asks for a third helping of chocolate pudding? "He looks so darling with chocolate all over his face" you say, "and he posed so nicely for the thirty pictures I took. Sure, he's starting to throw pudding on the floor and wall, but you know what? It's been a tough day. He got into a scuffle at Mothers-Day-Out. Some little heathen decided to hit him over the head for a toy, and that's the only reason my little trooper bit that awful monster. He's also been very upset that Grandma hasn't been by to see him today..." and on it goes.

We've all done the excuse thing too many times to count, having every justification in the world as to why our children would never act like "that" under normal circumstances. But guess what Mommy? LIFE is normal circumstances. It consists of glitches, hiccups, adversity, and hurdles. Schedules continually change, kids get sick and stay sick for what seems like half their toddlerhood, and Grandma misses a few visits here and there.

So let's stop being mushy about behavior. Our kids aren't always as well behaved as we would like. Big deal. Stop assuming you're a crappy parent if you admit your child's behavior drives you batty. Quit making excuses for being a punching bag! Behavior that drives you crazy is just that, and we've all been there. It doesn't mean you love your child any less. You're a great Mommy, so get over it.

What Exactly Are "Undesirable" Behaviors?

The subjective nature can be complicated. A good rule of thumb is that undesirable behavior is that which puts too much strain on you, your family, or your relationships. And you have to pay attention here, because other people see things Mommies do not. We tend to wear rose-colored glasses, getting very defensive where our offspring are concerned.

None of us live in a box, and we all know a child we'd describe as spoiled rotten or hateful. The parents, be they good by our standards or not, may acknowledge a particular behavior is present, but if it doesn't put enough of a burden on them, the child's behavior is acceptable – at least to them. This is a topic of curious debate in my monthly Poker Group. (We don't actually play poker, but it started out that way, so the name stuck.) My "Poker Mommies" as I call them, are a lovely group of ladies who share my fondness for toddlers. Presently we have a combined total of twelve kids under the age of six – and heaven help us, they just keep coming. My Poker friend Carey is perplexed as to how much behavior you can let go before you become a brat-maker. For instance, do you let your one-year-old throw a crayon across the room in frustration or do you nip that throwing business quickly?

Here are the general guidelines for unacceptable behavior:

1.   The behavior wears your nerves

2.   It disrupts or strains interaction with others

3.   It causes emotional or physical harm to any person or animal

4.   It causes destruction of property or objects

Keep in mind that behavior you think is okay may not really be okay. It's not okay for a child to endlessly scream in a public place. Even if your ears are numb and you no longer hear the wailing, it's disruptive to others. You may be too much of a pushover (I know, I'm harsh) to address the behavior, but other people and kids won't let you get away with it for long. You need to be considerate of others and pay attention. Otherwise, Aunt Muffy will stop coming by, former best friend Ashley will avoid you at all costs, and *your* little angel (unbelievable as it sounds) will be labeled a downright unpleasant child at preschool. Yikes!

Why We Give In and When to Stop

At the expense of being a squealer, let me enlighten you on a secret that no toddler or child would dare reveal for fear of being a traitor. When it comes to saying "no" or denying kids a 'want', they don't care nearly as much as they let on. Sure, it's a true sting to the soul to be denied chocolate, high heels, and a life-sized jeep, but toddlers have a short attention span. They'll forget all about it once you let them stir cake batter or spread jelly on bread. Don't believe a word of the moaning, groaning, griping, and growling when they don't get what they want. I promise they'll get over it.

Why is it we cave to demands and get our kids so much *stuff*? Is it some secret addiction we have to toys? Even if you're able to suppress your own squeals of delight when you hit the toy isle, you have to admit there's a certain cerebral high to loading up a basket full of doll clothes, snow cone makers, and dump trucks. And what about guilt? It can drive us to get our kids whatever their little heart desires. It's really no wonder when the yelling escalates to the point we're sure we were never meant to be parents. And those of you working 10 hour days with no extra time to give your children?... good grief. May as well hit that guilt button with fury! How could we shout at our kids like that? Why did we stay late at work and miss that gymnastics class? What kind of parents are we?!

Caregivers give in to a wide range of undesirable behavior. We're sappy, tired, divorced, stressed...the list is never ending. My husband frequently mentions that fighting is the last thing he wants to do with our girls when he has so little time with them as it is. As a weary and rushed parent, he sometimes feels it's easier to relent and give the little chick-a-dees what they want just to keep the peace. I beg to differ when he's getting fairly hacked off at our kids for drenching him with all the splashing in the bathtub. Is he having fun? Where's all the peace he keeps talking about?

When you feel irritated or resentful, take it as your clue that you're giving in too much and STOP. Toddlers are inspired and eternal optimists. They'll find creative avenues to get what they want and push you six ways from Sunday to get there. It's your child's lot in life to ask for more and poke around for limits. Give him some! Children need to know their boundaries. It gives them security and teaches respect and appreciation.

Personality Types and The Five Basics

All children need The Five Basics. Some kids just require more hands on help and time than others. For our purposes, we'll focus on the personality types that lend themselves to perceived behavior problems.

The Active/Energetic Child: So here we go. Raise your hand if you describe your love bug with terms like "lively", "energetic", or "active". That's code for wild. You and I both know it, so forget trying to fake me out. By nature of their need to be everywhere at once, active kids have a propensity to get overloaded and provisionally out of control. Sometimes this may necessitate one hundred percent of The Five Basics. I won't hoodwink you into thinking dishing out that much hands-on guidance is the easiest thing in the world, but it's not a monumental task either. You're putting in a gargantuan effort right now anyway, right? So let's utilize The Five Basics and make your life a heck of a lot easier.

If you're reluctant to address a behavior because (a) you don't know if it's normal for an active child and (b) you don't want to crush the incredible will of this type of personality, then determine if the behavior is something that's seriously wearing your nerves or causing you anguish. *Be honest.* Listen, I'm a supportive and agreeable gal, but if you start giving me a bunch of bogus excuses when you're clearly as strung out as a ball of yarn the cat just barfed up, you're not about to get a sympathetic ear. I'll simply nod and smile. Uh huh. Whatever.

The true active child is one that many consider to have special spirit. Being active does not automatically equal inappropriate or out of control. It just means that by nature of the need to skip around your house on a mission of destruction, active kids get out of control a bit quicker than your average kiddo. If you happen to have the liveliest child in the neighborhood, don't confuse the busy nature with behavior you find unacceptable. When a certain behavior pushes the brink of inappropriate, address it. You will absolutely not crush your child's special spirit. You will, in fact, give your toddler more security by giving her boundaries.

By and large, active kids need strict, consistent boundaries. But providing limits and being in control of the active child does not mean smothering - unless you want your batooty kicked. It's a losing battle to put an active child on a tight leash, so don't try. Just let the child know his boundaries (constantly, honey) so he'll feel secure. Pick your battles and remain consistent. Address and correct the most bothersome or disruptive issues. Give him a little more space on some of the less pressing (yet still annoying) behaviors.

Say your Pooh Bear likes to kick a ball in the backyard and get a little wild and aggressive. Let that be. Just make it clear that your backyard, by himself, is the ONLY time he can "kick the ball hard," or "yell at the ball." (Remember to give specifics on what is okay and not.) He needs to get that out of his system, but you need to make it clear that his boundaries are the backyard, alone. Starting to see? Allow the stimulus and expression of free spirit that active children need, but absolutely provide boundaries.

Active/Curious: These children aren't quite so hyper and destructive, but they still need constant activity and engagement. Often getting reprimanded for things like flooding the kitchen or setting the bed on fire, they seem to be quite the troublemakers. Probing and inquisitive, they ask five billion questions a day and talk nonstop. Or they may frequently engage in activities that are messy, dangerous, or all out nerve-wracking. This is just their way of learning. To keep them in control, they need guidance, consistency, and limits. Generally great kids, it often works well to talk them through points of curiosity. It may beat you to hell to answer "why does the sun shine?" questions all day long, but if you can muster up the stamina, engage them. Communicate your limits on answering questions and cleaning up after them. Make them respect those boundaries. But overall, try to embrace this personality type and go with the flow of their development.

Spirited Natures: These guys are feisty, smart and adorable – and won't hesitate to let you know when they're unhappy. My second two kids have this very spirited nature - happy and sweet, but definitely live wires. Spirited kids can be extremely whiny, demanding, and impatient, especially when sick or teething. When behavior turns sour, you have to provide gobs of limits and guidance. Those go-getting natures are a wonderful asset but can send you to Pluto. They need: outlets for the need to be active, alternatives to whining, instruction on how to control emotions instead of being demanding, and daily work on that forever unreachable concept of patience.

Generally Outrageous: Let's say your child is really much more along the lines of average. Does it mean you should have it easy? No way. Doling out just as much grief as a toddling tornado, these little critters torture the pet hamster and scream bloody murder when they get the pink frosted cookie instead of the white. It's also no biggie to wake up howling three times a night wanting water, then proceed to dump it all over their sheets and blankies...which leads to more howling.

Oh, and let's not forget the refusal to wear socks even if their tootsies are frozen, and the preoccupation with toilet paper. (What *is* it with eating those squares, wrapping baby sister up like a miniature mummy or stuffing it in the toilet until it's beyond repair? Drives me crazy!) The incessant whining, fussing, demanding, demolishing, and insistence on doing it "all by self!" along with the occasional punch in the face, kick in the stomach, or fleshy dental imprint from overactive chompers leaves no one in the clear. Every day, every hour, these guys need the Five Basics. Guidance on no-no's, limits to demands, structure for security, consistency on consequences, and communication help. Yep! You're not off the hook, so you can forget singing hosannas and praise, even with an "average" kid.

Severe and Chronic Undesirable Behaviors

Physical Cause: With problems bordering on severe or chronic, or if your child's behavior puts a hefty strain on your marriage and other relationships, my advice is to first rule out a physical cause such as illness, pain, or hearing loss. Get their hearing checked! I can't tell you how many times I hear "My three-year-old isn't talking yet and ignores me," or "He just won't listen to me," or "He doesn't seem to get what I'm saying." My first piece of advice is, maybe he can't! Make sure he can actually hear what you're telling him. Not three weeks ago, my friend Liz apologized to me after shouting at her toddler to stop running at the pool. "Sorry, I have to scream at her because she doesn't listen – literally can't hear me. We're going in next week to get tonsils and adenoids removed as well as [ear] tubes." Yea Liz for figuring that out! You rock!

When parents tell me speech is delayed or distorted, or the child yells when talking, or literally won't turn around when you call his name...red flags! Kids won't *make* sounds if they don't *hear* them. Or they'll talk really loud if they can't hear themselves clearly. Or they'll appear defiant when they seriously can't hear what you want. For an initial assessment, wait until your child's back is turned. Then pick some motivating item like his favorite string cheese or moon sand. In a completely normal voice volume, ask if he'd like some. See if he turns around. NO visual cues, either – like holding it up for him to see what you're talking about. If you do that, he'll put two and two together from the visual alone.

It's especially important to rule out a physical cause if the behavior is sudden in onset and you cannot link it to any emotional stress such as a new baby, new daycare, new house, or the like. My neighbor Janet once raced out of her house with wild eyes when she saw me walking down the street. She frantically begged for help because her child was acting completely out of character – screeching, attempting to climb walls, and breaking everything in sight. I told her to take little Bella to the doctor asap. Turned out she had Fifth disease and her joints were killing her. There you go. Pain!

Issues such as teething, sleep deprivation, diet, abuse, anxiety, or any number of troubles can contribute to behavioral problems. Sleep apnea or night terrors can make even the sweetest child psychotic. If you have no idea such things are going on or could be a factor, then it may very well seem that your child is just being obstinate or ill-behaved when they really are giving you clues on what they need. It may take a doctor's eye to catch a physical cause you never knew existed.

Sleep: Sleep deprivation is a biggie. That's why it's so important to treat any physical cause (give them Tylenol if their teeth hurt, people!). Or if the kid's running the show, it's imperative you change your behavior patterns and insist your child get proper sleep. When the day runs horrible and the only attention the child gets is at night, you'll *both* be kept up with pleas for snuggles, fighting, desperate wails for your presence, insistence on night lights, water, more books – you name it. Toddlers need about 12-13 hours of sleep each and every night. Surprised? Those are the statistics.

Food: Call me The Food-Nazi, but I must venture forth with my opinion. I mentioned diet earlier, really referring to allergic reactions to food, dyes, etc. However, when dealing with chronic behavior problems, take a look at the amount of sugar and processed food your kid gets. Candy, cookies, ice cream, and soda are obvious sources of ghastly behavior, but you have to look further. Cereal, juice, snacks (i.e., crackers, "fruit" chews, chips, cereal bars, etc.) are loaded with sugar. All those processed foods...ho-ly schmoly. SO bad for your kids! *Check food labels!* If the item has more than 5-10 grams of sugar per serving, pass it up. Plus, "partially hydrogenated" anything and "high fructose corn syrup" is crap-ola! Just plain bad.

You might be shocked and amazed how much sugar and *yuck* you've been giving your kid without even knowing it. Go through your pantry and fridge and THROW AWAY the garbage. That rubbish is nothing but boxes of behavior problems, girly! Try cutting back the sugar and processed junk by half and see if you notice a change in behavior. Then gradually cut it back even more.

You can certainly try to cut it cold turkey, but sugar is highly addictive, so be prepared for some fights. Nixing sugar completely can set off subsequent intense cravings and lead to some mighty big tantrums. You can use the sweeter fruits like oranges to substitute for the processed sugars. That might be enough to transition away without your kid needing rehab for withdrawal.

Go to the store and load up on foods that are <u>as close to their natural state as possible</u>. That means fruits and veggies. Organic stuff. And honey, I love ya, but you're a fool if you think you can keep eating gobbledygook, too. You are the role model. Clean up your act. Get a book by Dr. Oz or Dr. Andrew Weil; figure out what foods are most beneficial and healthy. Eat them. Make your kid eat them.

Now, it's my professional Mommy duty to throw in a bit of reality here and caution you not to jump on a physical cause as an automatic excuse for deplorable behavior. Once a doctor pronounces your little darling in perfect health, do your best to accept the advice and change your approach to the behavior to see if it will help. See a sleep specialist and nutritionist if needed. But after that, give it up. Your child isn't suffering an allergic reaction to mystical pollens, my dear. And listen, as a charter member of the Lame Excuse Club, I feel your pain. I once tried to justify horrific behavior on yogurt and cheap lemonade (although the crappy lemonade thing...I may have had a point). Anyway, rule out a physical cause. Beyond that, don't make crazy excuses for your kid's behavior.

ADD/ADHD: Ah, here it is. *"But my child has ADD!!"* Yeah, well, so do most of us adults. Attention Deficit (Hyperactivity) Disorder is, in my humble opinion, WAY over diagnosed. Does it exist? Of course. Absolutely, without question, a very real problem. But I would also submit that when you pair uneducated parenting with stupid food, you'll see some awfully similar symptoms. Let's see what all these 'ADD kids' have in their lunchbox, eh? And take a gander at how the parents reinforce the behaviors. My guess is that a good chunk of these kids would have a significant decrease in symptoms if those two factors were turned upside down.

ADD has very specific, neurological components. True ADD kids exhibit symptoms way out of the norm of age-appropriate behaviors. Their poor brains are on overload *nonstop*. The impossibility of organizing and categorizing all that information and input is heartbreaking. These kids do the best they can to function in society, with no idea that what they see, hear, and process is entirely different from the rest of us. ADD does exist and it's devastating. My point is (a) don't compound the problem by ineffectual nutrition and parenting or (b) label the behavior 'ADD' simply because we can't change our habits and face up to the behavior <u>we</u> created. Harsh, I know, but that's me. Sorry Charlie! It'd be a waste of time and cowardly to reinforce detrimental habits simply because it's what you want to hear.

So What's Normal? Excluding those behaviors attributed to physical triggers (or mystical, magical, or supernatural, just to cover all the bases) defining normalcy eludes those of us constantly engulfed in toddler craziness. Do normal toddlers go for days on end eating nothing but bananas or peanut butter sandwiches? Or let loose a river of pee all over the floor of Borders Books and Chili's?

Normalcy itself is redefined in the dwelling place of a toddler. Who, other than the Mommy of a two-foot tall poop machine, would consider it normal to fish out floating feces from the bathtub every other day? I do recall the days when I could not begin to fathom the logistics of that particularly disgusting chore, but since one of my daughters tends to make it a habit (no names since she'll eventually grow up and hate me for it), it's no big deal now. *("Where's the box of gloves, honey?!")*

At times our kids are so demanding that we can't take five minutes to shovel down a bowl of oatmeal without little people hanging on our legs, throwing a crying convention. Don't you swear there are days when your kids spend half their waking hours with tears streaming down their face and mouths cranked open, pathetically wailing for one reason or another? Is all this normal? Who knows? Just don't let your toddler take over your household because you don't want to interfere with "the norm". "Normal" doesn't necessarily have to mean "acceptable". You decide what's tolerable for you and your family.

Chapter Two Review: What Did We Learn?

YOU have the power to turn negative behavior around.

Definition of Undesirable Behaviors.

Why parents give in so much.

Personality types:

- Active/Energetic

- Active/Curious

- Spirited natures

Four causes of severe and chronic behavior problems in normally developing children.

Chapter Three: Changing Our Communication

Oooo, how we cringe hearing the word *discipline*. The word itself has a horribly bad rap. But in actuality, it's not so dreadful. The word "discipline" means to learn or teach. For our purposes, we'll add on "development of self control" and we have a fairly dog-gone accurate description of what we're talking about: Discipline as a means **to teach development of self-control.** And rest easy; this does not include aversive (another of Dr. Chandler's favorite words) punishment or responses.

True and loving discipline is far removed from cruelty or barbaric forms of punishment. In fact, spanking, swatting, pinching, hitting, slapping, flicking your fingers on your child's head, or anything involving physical punishment is absolutely not necessary! Besides, how would you feel if someone bopped you on the butt for putting too much salt in the meatloaf or letting the car run out of gas? Kids are innocent, vulnerable, and impressionable. All loving Mommies know that using harsh physical means to punish or correct a child's behavior leave us feeling so guilty that it overrides any luck we might have had with the method.

Good news. You don't have to use physical punishment anymore. Yea! No spanking necessary! Our positive approaches yield the results you seek and stop the cycle of reinforcing attention for undesirable behaviors.

Control

Here's the truth: When toddlers get everything they want and run the household, they're out of control. Toddlers need YOU to hold the reins of freedom and set parameters. As much as they protest to the contrary, toddlers cannot deal with getting everything they want. There are too many choices and too much freedom. Their little baby brains cannot handle the lack of restrictions and they'll go into overload. Mommies often try and appease their little ones by giving in to every whine and cry thinking this will make the kiddo happy. Here's the thing: _toddlers don't know what they need_. They certainly know what they _want_, but this is altogether different than needs. Giving in to demands will not make your child happy. It will make him out of control.

The reason toddlers continually ask for more is to <u>secure limits.</u> Read that sentence again and highlight it!! Dog-ear this page! You set yourself up for undesirable behavior if you give your child six toothbrushes, four cereals, and nine shirts to choose from each morning, because it's _too much_ for him. Toddlers need limited choices. It makes them feel safe.

Honoring the Gift

To discipline your child is to love her and accept the gift of life you've been given. An old priest of mine once told a story about a guitar he received as a gift from a church member. Father Henry thanked the person for being so nice and thoughtful, then proceeded to watch the instrument collect dust in the corner of his office. The problem was, he didn't actually know how to play the guitar. Another priest eventually asked him about it. Father Henry said he wasn't sure why that church member gave him the guitar, but he didn't want to be rude and say, "No thank you, I don't play." The enlightening response from the other priest was, "Then you haven't truly accepted the gift." If Father Henry had truly accepted the guitar, he would have learned how to play the instrument and honored the true meaning of the gift. The same goes for our toddlers. _**To truly accept the gift of our children, we must honor what it takes to raise them.**_

I remember a distraught Mommy tearfully telling me she didn't discipline enough because she didn't want to seem ungrateful for the precious gift she'd been given. Although her child's behavior was overwhelming, the Mommy felt cruel when using any discipline. She understood her daughter was a gift, but *mis*understood what it meant to accept the gift. In order to truly accept the treasure of a baby's life, one must honor what it takes to raise the child. Honor means respect and love. Love means guidance on issues such as self-control. Self-control requires discipline. Accepting the gift means saying 'no' sometimes and instructing your child on how to successfully negotiate through life.

Teaching children that you get whatever you want if you throw enough fits is not being honest with them. It doesn't teach them what life is really about. As an adult in this society, honor and respect are revered. It's not honorable or respectful to mow down other adults or cuss them out in our attempt to make a point or get what we want. If we give our children what they want whenever they throw a fit, it sends the wrong message and teaches them that whining, badgering, and yelling is okay and acceptable – which is not true. If we are not honest with our children, we are not *honoring* the gift we have been given.

Discipline Starts With Time Management

It's absolutely amazing how much time children need. Even the little bitties! You'd think being able to put an infant down somewhere and have them stay put would be a blessing. But even those tiny creatures require constant hands on care. My sweet veterinarian once told me that after the birth of her son, she couldn't wait for her maternity leave to end so she could get back to work and "rest."

Bladder howling, one time my friend Julie tried "telling" her five-week-old (oh, that cracks me up!) that she needed to go, but little Meagan wouldn't hear of it. (Really? How strange.) Asking and begging was unsuccessful (duh), so she finally put woefully-unhappy-Meagan in her swing where she knew the baby would be safe, and ran off to the bathroom yelling, "You need to stay there and entertain yourself because I HAVE GOT TO GO!" But Julie's husband Steve wasn't brave enough to leave their little princess alone when he needed to go. No sir-ee. Putting Meagan in her carrier, he'd plop her down in the open bathroom doorway, tending to his potty business as he and babydoll exchanged silent, solemn stares.

The most essential aspect of time management is learning how to read toddler needs and use your time most efficiently to meet those needs. When a Mommy spends loads of time and effort getting her child to do the most basic daily rituals, it means that needs are not being met and time is being wasted. Forget using the potty, love. Might as well pee your pants. Toddlers have their own timetable and mission of discovery, but the struggle for independence should not involve making your life miserable and forcing you to use Depends.

Spending all free time skirmishing with your toddler just sucks. Then you start letting undesirable behavior slide because you're too tired to fight, right? It may seem like a monumental task to take the time now and put in the effort to change, but really, what are you doing anyway? Aren't you already spending most of your time dealing with your child? Make the most of the time you already spend. *Put it toward The Five Basics of* **structure, communication, limits, consistency, and guidance.** Make your child *secure and happy.* This means you will have *more* time in the future because you won't be spending every other minute in warfare with your toddler.

Let's say, for instance, little Bobby takes fifteen minutes to brush his teeth. Why so long? Does he fiddle around for five minutes trying to decide which of the twelve fascinating brushes to choose from? If so, he's overloaded and needs some limits. Eliminate the fiddle time by donating eleven toothbrushes to your local garbage can and give him ONE to pick. Simplicity in choice makes it darn easy. Then, give him some structure and set a routine for brushing his teeth.

First, decide who puts paste on the brush (I vote for the adult). Determine who turns on the water and wets the brush. Then, give the actual brushing task a sequence. My husband, Chris, gives our daughters four steps – "up, down, eee (cleaning the front teeth), and aaah (cleaning the tongue)". Each and every time our children brush their teeth, Chris says, "up...down...eee...ah" and helps with the four steps. We provide this guidance and structure so our children know what to expect and what they're supposed to do.

The key to increasing cooperation and making time work for you is to get a routine, provide guidance and limits, and BE CONSISTENT. And part of being consistent is making sure every caregiver follows the exact same steps. My husband made sure I was on board with his tooth-brushing system when he started it. He knew that if I did it differently, it would ruin the consistency and make the task confusing. Using the tooth-brushing example, let's set up a working TAG; the kind that consistently promotes positive behavior:

A: You say, "Time to brush your teeth."

B: Child gets his *one* toothbrush; you put on paste and give consistent cues; child completes task appropriately

C: (**R**) You tell child "Great job brushing!"

When you keep the task simple, give clear instructions on what you want, be consistent with your prompts/cues, and praise your child for a job well done, you've just reinforced the behavior you want. Woohoo!

Task Analysis

All this breaking down of activities and giving steps is what Dr. Chandler defines as **Task Analysis.** It's a way to break down tasks into individual parts so the overall activity isn't so overwhelming. When the task is overwhelming, overload kicks in. Makes sense, right? So really think about the activity; list all components of the task in the order in which they must be performed. If need be, go through a simple task yourself such as putting on shoes and socks. Break down the activity into steps: Get socks. Get shoes. Sit down. Weave fingers through first sock. Put toes into sock. Pull sock on. Straighten sock. And so forth. See how many steps are actually taken? Sit back and figure out which of these steps your child can actually do and which ones he needs work on. If he can't physically perform step 4, then the entire task falls apart. So work on step 4 outside of the task itself.

Example: Junior balks at washing his hands. Every time you stick his hands in the sink, he goes limp, cries and kicks. What's going on? Step back and take a look at the big picture. Can he reach the sink without your help? Can he turn on the water? Use the soap pump? Do you nag him about his nails every time you see dirt? All these steps can be overwhelming. So break it down. Cut out the nonessentials like nagging or insisting he hang the towel back up. You can work on that later. Of the essential steps, see what he has the most trouble with – then help him master the step. Once mastered, put the rest of the steps together in a consistent and structured manner. Go through each step with him and *say* the same things every time. *Do* the same things every time.

You cannot teach independence with complex sequences until you figure out what you want to teach and break it down into component parts. After that, you can begin to see what areas need work, and figure out which cues and prompts will best help your child learn. Cues and prompts are essential to training kids how to perform tasks and behave appropriately.

Prompting

Prompting is any assistance given by a caregiver to promote correct responding. It's all about eliciting behavior without mistakes or frustration. When done the right way, **prompting increases the**

likelihood that a child will do what you want or ask. We do it every day without even thinking:

- Hold our hand out wanting child to take it.

- Saying, "put your arm in here" while helping them get dressed.

- Touching their back to prompt them forward.

- Patting a surface indicating 'sit'.

Prompts are instructions, gestures, demonstrations, touches, or other things we do to help children make correct responses. **There are five types of prompts: Verbal, Modeling, Gesture, Physical, and Visual.**

Verbal: Verbal prompts are words, instructions, or questions meant to direct a child to do something particular. Important: **verbal prompts are the least effective!** This is why parents get so frustrated with their toddlers; there are too many verbal prompts given the wrong way. We talk too much! Too many steps, too much direction, or constant yammering only confuses the poor kid.

For example, when getting dressed, the parent will yak, yak: "Put on your shirt. Take those pants off, they don't match. Put the blue ones on instead. Put on these socks." ...and so forth. Then the parent wonders why the heck the kid can't dress himself when the task has been reiterated four hundred times. It's too much information to process, and the instructions are inconsistent.

Here are some examples of verbal prompts:

- "Do you want to eat?"

- "Let go of the book."

- "Hold still."

- "I told you to stop that!" (This prompt is nonspecific and does not work. Unfortunately, we do it all the time!)

Modeling: Modeling demonstrates a response and it's generally used in conjunction with other prompts.

- Caregiver says, "Do you want to eat?" as she acts out eating. (model + verbal)

- Caregiver says, "Open the door" as she opens the door for the child. (model + verbal)

Gesture: Gestural prompts consist of pointing, motioning, or nodding toward the child, objects, materials, or activities indicating an action to be performed. These are also used with other prompts. Examples:

- "Do you want to eat?" Point to bottle or cracker. (gestural + verbal)

- "Open the door." Point to door. (gestural + verbal)

Physical: Physical prompts are physical contact from a caregiver that demonstrates what you want (something functional like showing them how to tie a shoe). This includes hand over hand, escorting, hand on shoulder, hand on elbow, hand on wrist, or any other touch. Physical prompts require the most hands-on help, but research indicates **these prompts work the best.** When you give physical prompts, you walk the child through the activity.

These prompts are not only the best type to use, but also easier to fade. For example, you can use these along with verbal cues. Then, as the child understands and demonstrates the task and sequence, you can stop using so many physical prompts and stick to the verbal prompts to walk them through (only as needed) until they are independent.

Example of a physical prompt:

- "Stack the blocks like this." Take child's hand and show him how to stack blocks.

Visual: This prompt is most often used when attempting to get a verbal response of some sort. They include written words, pictures, objects, people and places. You'll find these prompts hanging on walls in preschool classes (calendars, alphabet, etc.) or made into a book to help nonverbal kids talk or communicate. (A little speech therapy there.) Or they can be a building or object in the environment. Examples:

- Show the child a picture of Daddy and say, "Who's that?"

- Drive up to a McDonalds and ask, "Where are we?"

- Hold up a toothbrush and inquire, "What do you do with this?"

Using Prompts

Toddlers require prompting all the livelong day. We just usually do it wrong and promptly get furious when we get a negative response. Study the different prompts. Figure out which ones you're using. If you find that you're sticking only to verbal, change your habits. Use more physical prompts and modeling for difficult activities. And girly, this means actually putting down your coffee (nooooooo!), getting up, and showing your toddler exactly what you want done and how. I promise, correctly using physical (and other) prompts will cut the learning time in half. When you give kids hands on training for certain tasks, the probability they'll pick it up sooner and start doing it independently increases dramatically. This takes more time and effort up front, but the decrease in later frustration is fantastic!

Sign Language

One of THE biggest problems getting through the toddler years is lack of communication. As a speech therapist, you find out quickly that it's the basis for most behavior problems you run into during therapy. And as a mom, you figure out all too soon that you're clueless most of the time: Your toddler wants milk, not juice. He's tired; doesn't want to rock. Teeth are the problem, not a stomachache. No, little baby doll doesn't want peas, she wants crackers. On and on it goes. How many times a day do we fret over WHAT IS WRONG WITH YOU? Sometimes we know, most of the time we don't. We guess. We're wrong, so we try again. Oooo, we got a swat that time, so that can't be it. Let's try something else. Okay, you're not interested in the keys or remote control, so I give up! Cry your heart out; I'm stumped!

You can head off so many problems and headaches by teaching your child Sign Language. Even five or ten signs can make a world of difference cutting out the whining and fussing. Start with the very basic one-year-old needs: milk, eat, finished, sleep, more, help, bath, binky. Once you get those down, expand: banana, cracker, water, juice, duck, bird, ball, dog, cheese. It's absolutely stunning how much a *baby* knows and cannot tell you for lack of ability to talk. At all of twelve months old, one of my kids pointed to her empty bottle one night and signed, 'milk, eat, finished, sleep'. She was essentially telling me, "I'm finished with my food and bottle; now I'm full and it's time for bed."

Teaching your child sign language opens up doors for communication. A child that can't *tell* you what she's thinking but can *sign* what she's thinking is an altogether different child. And toddlers *are* thinking, I promise. They know what they want, how they feel, and they process thoughts; they just can't convey it. Problem solving. Thinking. Processing. She can do it all. She just can't tell you. Teach her some signs and she will.

Kids acquire language and begin talking in a wide range. Every kid is different. How they react to and pick up signs will vary. One kid can have 100 signs by the time she's two, yet another will barely use any because she's talking early and doesn't need them to communicate. You won't know if they're going to be 'talkers' until they hit about 12 months, so go ahead and start teaching signs. At the very least, you'll always use the basic starter signs. The best time to start teaching Sign Language is about 8 months old or when they demonstrate the ability to wave bye-bye. That's a sign, and it tells you they associate hand movements with actions or objects, and they have the appropriate motor skills.

To introduce a sign, use it each and every time you get out the object and present it to your child. "Milk" is always the best first sign because it's a basic and common need. When your child begins indicating a need for a bottle or breast, present it while signing and saying "milk". Use physical prompts and manipulate their hands to show them how to make the sign. (Remember, physical prompts are the most effective, especially when teaching Sign Language.) After you manipulate their hands, give the milk *immediately* so they associate the sign with the activity/object. Over time you can eventually fade the prompts. Ideally, to get what they want, they must do something functional; sign instead of cry or fuss – even if it's only you manipulating their hands to make the sign. The most important point here is to **be consistent**. Otherwise you'll just confuse them. Keep it up and have faith.

Now, always the one to throw a wrench into the technically correct, I have a bit to add here. As a Mommy currently going through this signing business (a-*gain*) I must interject and allow you to fudge the steps. Sometimes your child will get mighty angry with you. If he's starving, frustrated, or out of control and crying furiously, you can occasionally forget about the physical prompt. Make the sign yourself and quickly meet the need. When he calms down, and if the object is still the main focus (i.e., he's still drinking his bottle), you have another opportunity and can try to manipulate his hands if you like. But don't tick him off. Just bear in mind that next time you must examine the **A** in the Toddler ABC Guide and set up the situation better.

Don't wait until he's aggravated beyond control before you start the task or meet the need. Rather, attempt the physical and verbal prompts when you know your child is receptive. It may take several weeks (or in rare cases a month or two) until they finally start signing independently, but they will. And the sweetness of seeing your baby sign...uh! Makes my heart pitter-pat to think of it!

Once you get the starter signs down, get online or hit your local bookstore and pick up any old book on baby signs. And if the signs are too complex, modify them so your baby's hands can actually make them. For instance, I've found that the sign for "ball" is too difficult and needs to be modified. However, sometimes a child will automatically modify the signs and you can just follow their lead. "Finished" usually ends up as simply flapping hands up and down, which is fine. And "balloon" and "binky" are completely made up in my house. Making up and modifying signs is okay, as long as they're specific, and all caregivers understand the sign in context. My first kid used the same sign (that she made up) for "video" and "cheerios", but given context, I always knew what she wanted, and it didn't matter. My third kid makes "blanket" and "bath" look pretty much the same, but who really cares? Keep your eye on the big picture; communicating quickly, easily, and efficiently. That's what counts.

Here are some basic signs for you to begin with:

Finished: Palms up, then flip down

Bath: Move fists up and down body as if scrubbing

Milk: Open and close fist as if milking a cow

Eat: Closed fingers to mouth

Binky/Pacifier: Example of a modified sign: Index finger to mouth

Help: Open left palm; right fist on palm

More: Fingers together

Sleep/Bed

One last note about teaching signs; don't bother with "yes" and "no". It
may seem terribly obvious to you that they can actually shake their
head for these two signs, but you'd be surprised how you're thinking
clouds when you're trying something new. I once walked into an ICU
room to evaluate a patient who had recently suffered a stroke and
couldn't talk or communicate. His well-intentioned and loving family
had already started a method of squeeze-my-hand-once-for-yes-and-
twice-for-no. Imagine their surprise when I asked the patient questions
to which he shook his head "yes" and "no". Once I determined that he
was answering questions appropriately and hadn't suffered brain
damage affecting his basic comprehension, I told the family that hand
squeezing to communicate "yes" and "no" wasn't necessary. Besides,
those two signs are too difficult for toddler hands to master.

To wrap up, I'll answer the burning question I just know you're dying to ask: Does using Sign Language delay speech? My answer is no. Going on sheer experience, kids will acquire language and speech when they acquire language and speech. Period. They will stop signing when it becomes easier for them to talk to communicate needs. If a language or speech problem exists, it's going to exist from the get-go. It's just how babies are wired when they pop out. We can either help them along or hinder the process. Teaching Sign Language helps children communicate faster. In doing so, needs are met and kids stay happy. Can you imagine how trapped a child feels when language or speech is already delayed and they have no way to communicate except crying and pointing? Go ahead and pour me a cup of Pepto because that sucks! I've seen it in action, and everyone loses.

If you have a child whose language and speech is right on track, teaching them signs to communicate will not hinder the ability to talk and acquire language. They will do it when they're ready. Just to prove I'm all heart, my first kid did end up in speech therapy (the end-all confession, as I am a speech therapist), but it had nothing to do with signing. She signed better than any kid I've ever seen, but her language was delayed. (FYI, language and speech are different. Basically, *language* is the process their brain goes through to organize and put thoughts and words together. *Speech* – or articulation – is the actual placement of their tongue to make the correct sounds or pronunciation of words.) My daughter's language was an issue from the beginning. As a speech therapist and new Mommy, my blabbing mouth was never far from her ears, filling them with language. And yet, she was still delayed. My child needed speech therapy, but I never blamed it on signing. In fact, signing saved her from immense frustration. Today she's totally fine (three cheers for speech therapists!) with no further language issues.

Now. Reality. If your child is used to signing and it works for him, that's what he'll do until it's easier to talk than sign. And listen up...this is okay!! Don't freak out. The goal here is communication – get it done however you can. If you get worried as he creeps up on 24-30 months, go to your local school district or private speech therapist and have him evaluated. It will either ease your mind, or get him into needed therapy. Win – win. Look, I get just as antsy as the next Mommy, fretting and anxious that my child will be forever mute. But seriously, it just doesn't happen that way. They will learn to talk, and before we know it they'll be mouthing off, making us want to scream. So if you're worried, dive into the process and educate yourself. If not, sign away and be happy!

Chapter Three Review: What Did We Learn?

Definition of discipline and control.

Why giving in to demands won't work.

Why toddlers continually ask for more.

How to honor the gift of our children.

How to management your time and increase cooperation.

How to use Task Analysis to increase understanding and cooperation.

Five types of prompts and how to use them:

1. Verbal

2. Modeling

3. Gesture

4. Physical

5. Visual

Eight starter signs to increase communication.

Part II: Application

Chapter Four: Promoting Positive Behavior

Little Maggie flings herself to the ground in the middle of the mall and commences with *"Nooooooo! Don't want chicken! Want ice creeeaammm!"*

Oh dear, not now. Why, *why* does this always happen in public? Why can't this child save the ballistic nonsense for someplace that doesn't have five hundred pairs of eyes scrutinizing the lack of parental control? Letting out a huge sigh of defeat, you do the only reasonable thing. You give in. "Okay, okay! We'll get some ice cream! Just calm down!" Yes, you know you shouldn't be doing this, but heck, what are your options? Grab a seat and casually watch your child tirade for the next ten minutes?

Any realistic parent will tell you there are times when toddlers act so horrible that you'd like find the nearest hole and bury your head. Even if the antics closely resemble that of a wild boar, sometimes it just isn't feasible to pack up and go home. What are you supposed to do then? For those who suffer frequent mortification, where on earth do you even begin?

Trust, Security, and Control

If you want to increase cooperation and nix the exasperating outbursts, set up an environment of trust, security, and control. How? Here's where to begin:

1. Start With Respect. Give respect and expect respect. Respect your toddler's routine. If naptime is two o'clock, stop shopping and get them home and in bed by two. If you don't chose to be respectful of your child's needs, don't expect your little muffin to be gracious and refrain from slinging grape juice all over the $200 nighties while you drag him around Victoria's Secret. It's also not respectful to others to make them listen to your little darling whine and cry while you shop. When I finally get the rare chance to shop without my kids, I certainly don't want to listen to someone else's!

While I understand your plight, I'm really more sympathetic to the tired and hungry little guy who's being forced to endure his feet being stuffed into five different pairs of shoes with no end in sight. Give him a break! He'll live another day without new shoes! If it's that important, work around *his* schedule and chose a time when he's fed and well rested before you force him to endure such a boring activity.

2. No Yelling. No matter how upset you are or how bad the crime, when you yell, you have lost control. Then bad things happen: (a) kids stop listening, and (b) you give negative attention. When you yell at your child, they quickly realize what a power trip it is to get you so worked up. If you want to maintain control, stay in command of your emotions. Keep your volume and tone down.

Granted, there are exceptions to the rule. Whacking you on the head with a golf club or running into the street yields a knee jerk yell. And really, it's just an innate protection mechanism – your brain and their life. Exceedingly atrocious acts aside, yelling in general for things like getting them to stop hollering in the car (the epitome of irony) or for pouring orange juice into the fireplace, is not the correct way to diminish undesirable behavior.

Now, wrapping up the yelling lecture, let me throw in a bit of reality. Even the best of us occasionally find ourselves howling at the moon - and our toddlers. If you can keep your voice down about 90% of the time, give yourself a congratulatory pat on the back. I haven't met a Mommy yet who has mastered vocal composure, so don't dog yourself if you haven't either. (And please don't write to me and gloat if you have. I have enough to feel guilty about!)

3. Model Desirable Behaviors. Model the behavior you want your toddler to demonstrate. When making a request of a little person, always put "please" in there, and reward him with a "thank you" when he complies. Treat your child and others around you (that means Daddy too!) with respect and gratitude, because I guarantee, toddler eyes are watching!

Make life one big modeling session. Whatever you do and wherever you go, model what you want to see, and exaggerate it a bit. For example, if you want Johnny-toddler to be nice to baby brother, model specific behaviors. When you handle the baby, pick him up gently and say, "We must be very gentle with babies. See how Mommy holds him gently? He loves for you to pat his back like this. Now you try." Take Johnny's hand. Using a physical prompt, show him how light of a touch you want. Afterward, praise and make sure he knows how pleased you are. Give him extra kisses for being so sweet. He will eventually get the drift that he gets positive attention when he's kind to baby brother. In addition, repeating the word "gentle" teaches him what you mean when you use the word. "Gentle" is a difficult and abstract concept for toddlers to understand unless you consistently demonstrate.

Always model the behavior you want to see and be careful about behavior you don't want to see! Toddlers have a very shrewd way of displaying our worst habits. It'll happen at some point, so either clean up your act or close your eyes and cross your fingers that your little one won't find a beer can at the park and proudly present it to Grandma saying, "Daddy's water!" (And you just know it'll be *your* mother, not your mate's. Toddlers are way too fun loving to miss an opportunity to embarrass the tar out of us.)

One of the sparkling jewels your toddler gives is a check on how you're treating him and others. So catch it when you find yourself snapping, "hush!" to your baby, or big sister will start doing the same. Little children do what they observe and give back what they are given. Start showing them and others the respect you wish to get. Your little copycat will eventually start meowing just like you, and there's nothing more heart melting than getting a sweet kiss with, "Tanks! I lub you, Mama".

4. Provide Structure and Routine. Schedules need to be consistent. I CANNOT STRESS THIS ENOUGH. Daily and weekly activities should be fairly predictable. Some kids are more flexible than others, but for the most part, they love routines. Toddlers feel in control and happy when daily schedules and bedtime routines are consistent. It works best when you keep the time and the routine the same.

Keep naptime and bedtime the same EVERYDAY. Sleep schedules need to be absolutely predictable. For example, consistently put Jr. down for a nap at one o'clock. Sing a song, read one book, and give a naptime kiss. At bedtime, have another routine – bath at seven, brush teeth, and two stories while cuddling on Daddy's lap. Do not – I repeat – DO NOT read four books one night, two the next, and keep changing up the routine. Remember, toddlers want to know their boundaries. Two books means two books. Period.

If you think he's getting shafted on reading time, read more books during playtime throughout the day. When it comes to bedtime, you CANNOT continually deviate and give in to repeated requests. No matter how sweet and endearing the plea, you say "No." Otherwise, don't start feeling sorry for yourself when you wake up one day and realize you've got some hefty sleep issues on your hands. You make your own bed when you neglect to give your child a firm, loving, and consistent routine to wrap him up in security.

When it comes to sleep schedules, do not deviate and let toddlers stay up late. Forget about lax bedtime on weekends or waiting for Daddy to get home from work. And don't try to run your children around in order to tire them out. It only makes them *over* tired, throwing them way off track. Keep the transition easy by making activities before bedtime or naptime calm, relaxing, and consistent. **Structure and routine give toddlers security**.

Guide them to stay on task during sleep routines. Let them know if they don't finish bath or brush teeth timely, there won't be time for the fun stuff, like reading books or having Daddy 'check their ears' for treats. No cooperation, no fun stuff. NO EXEPTIONS. And understand going in, they *will* test you. Expect to send them to bed heartbroken a time or two. They'll be much more cooperative from then on. If not, put your foot down again. No cooperation means you're giving in somewhere and they know it. Start being consistent. Give them security. I swear to Pete, the first time they actually give you a kiss goodnight, smile, and go right to sleep, you'll freak with wonder and love. It's a great feeling, girl!

5. Repetition of Rules. Toddlers don't have the attention span or memory to keep up with all the tedious laws of etiquette and safety, so you must repeat, and repeat, until you're absolutely sure your head will explode. I know it's difficult to restate yourself so much that you slur, but repetition of rules is very important and you must be consistent. Be patient and prepare to say the same things twelve gazillion times.

Try to remember where your kids are coming from. Don't take it personally when they can't remember that forks aren't for eye poking and Q-tips don't go in your nose. I've been regurgitating the same phrases for so many years now that my teeth are ground to nubs, but I still keep up with, "We don't dump Mommy's CD's on the floor," and "We don't play in Mommy's cabinets" fifty times a day. Knowing you must endure a lifetime (okay, so it just *seems* like a lifetime) of repetition may not prepare your sanity for the marathon, but at least you won't step onto the course blind. Take it day by day, keeping that calming herbal tea handy. (And feel free to spike it every once in a while – but you didn't hear that from me.)

6. The Two Rules of Engagement. Whenever I'm in the grocery store or mall and hear a Mommy snarl out, "If you do that *one more time...*" I just crack up! What a crock! Maybe I'm out of the loop of super moms and obedient wonders, but these peepers have yet to witness kids straighten up and stand at attention when Mommy fires off that cannon.

To avoid lame and useless threats, you must say what you mean and do what you say.

Say What You Mean

Say what you mean, *consistently*. When you give your child a consequence, say what you mean and make it something you can live with. You must have every intention of following through. I've heard "If you don't stop now, we will leave!" so many times it makes my head spin. Yet I have never once witnessed Mom or Dad sling the kicking, screaming kid over their shoulder and head out the door after the threat. Not once, not ever. Do you think this tells Dennis the Menace that Mommy and Daddy mean business? Absolutely not! It's telling him precisely what's going on - that Mom and Dad paid a hefty admission fee to the local Water World, or the pizza hasn't arrived yet at Pee Wee's Pizza Palace. They have no intention of doing anything other than spewing out a few choice words. Big whoop.

Do What You Say – No Idle Threats

Kids respond to your promises if they know you aren't kidding. Tell them the consequence to any continued behavior and give them time to comply. If they choose not to cooperate, implement your consequence. DO NOT GIVE IDLE THREATS!! Do not even think about letting it slide so you can continue organizing your closet. Idle threats are a Mommy's worst enemy because it means a child has no limits. Stop what you're doing, get up, and go through with your consequence – every time, consistently. If you promise a Popsicle as a reward for taking a good nap, hold to it. Don't be a sissy. A two-hour session of popping out of bed every six minutes does not equal "good nap". Believe me, he'll pitch a fit, but if you told him he had to actually *sleep* for the reward, hold to your word and refuse that Popsicle. I promise, he'll remember it next time. You may have one helluva afternoon, but don't wimp out! You can make it.

The rules of engagement build a foundation of trust. For example, if "five more minutes" or "one more time" doesn't seem to work for you, assess whether you're saying what you mean and doing what you say. If your child doesn't trust you, she'll consistently be aggressive and obstinate when the five minutes are up. And you can't blame the kid. It's more likely you've taught her "five more minutes" just means she has to turn on the voice, water works, and kickboxing moves to get what she wants. She knows darn well that you singing, "Five more minutes, Boo Boo!" means she's got a good forty five minutes of play as long as she's strategic. Transitions are difficult enough as it is. Don't compound the problem by being inconsistent with your follow through.

Demanding behavior means you are: Inconsistent, giving too much, and not setting limits.

Go through with what you say. Being a sucker teaches your child that you're not trustworthy. When you cannot be trusted to go through with what you say, then things like "I'll get it in a minute" and "I'll be right back" mean nothing. Be honest when telling your child time frames. Make sure that "five more minutes on the slide" really means five more minutes on the slide. If you are leaving your child with a sitter, don't tell her you'll only be gone a few minutes. That's dishonest and unfair. It's confusing when five minutes on the slide doesn't come anywhere near the five minutes with a sitter. When toddlers don't trust your word, tantrums, clingy behavior, separation anxiety, and bedtime battles are imminent. Honesty, consistency, and limits give toddlers security.

Power Phrases

Language is powerful, and the language you use can make or break your success with behavior modification. The following power phrases let children know what is expected of them, what comes next, and what they're supposed to be doing. Use these all the time to promote security and control.

"It's time to…" or "It's not time to…"

This is an excellent compliment to a structured environment. Having a sense of daily events puts toddlers in control, and they love it. When they have a basic routine to follow, it creates less resistance when a change of activity is in order (i.e., "It's time to eat lunch" or "It's time to leave the park now"). When naptime rolls around and your toddler runs to play with her favorite puzzle, a sentence like "It's not time to play with the puzzle; it's time for your nap" lets her know what's expected for that particular time of day. Even if you use this phrase for an unscheduled event like riding the display bikes in the local toy store ("It's time to stop riding the bike now and come with Mommy"), it'll help your toddler realize there's a time for everything, and now is the time to stop.

"You may…"

Instead of telling kids what they cannot have or play with, tell them what they CAN have or play with. Examples:

1. Little Trevor wants another sandwich for lunch but still has an entire uneaten bowl of soup:

> Instead of saying: No! Finish what you've got.

> Say: The sandwich is gone. You may finish your soup.

2. He's driving you crazy with a push toy:

> Instead of saying: Stop that!

> Say: You may play with the blocks or the coloring books. (Redirection)

Giving toddlers limited choices on what they CAN do eliminates a bossy demand by you and provides a positive choice of action.

As a therapist at an elementary school, I once had to work with a particularly difficult set of twin boys. Sprinting down the halls, dashing into bathrooms, and insisting on sampling the water at every single fountain, it took their mother about ten minutes just to get them to the speech room. With the attention span of a fly and no sense of boundaries, rules, or authority, they had absolutely no clue they weren't the center of the universe. Kelly, my supervisor (and Mommy friend), was simply wonderful in showing me how to keep them under control.

Because these boys were especially challenging, the first thing we had to do was establish our authority. Kelly began the process by giving them only two things they could do for the duration of the thirty-minute session. We spent the entire time repeating, "You may jump, or you may play in the balls." Eyes crossed and woozy from all the repetition, I had to brace a kiddie chair to keep from falling over.

Lo and behold, it really worked to give these boys structure and consistent redirection when they tried to deviate from the limited choices. It only took two therapy sessions for us to prove our role as leader and gain their trust. The end result was increased cooperation. From that point on, they knew what was expected and they felt in control. When it was time for a structured activity, they were much more accommodating to my requests. I still had to continually give them limited choices and constantly redirect, but using "You may..." really helped. I would tell them, "It's not time to play with the blocks; you may sit at the desk and glue the shapes onto the paper." These boys needed loads of positive guidance and responded well to this technique.

"We (do)..." "We do not..."

These phrases let children know how to behave in certain situations. The little love bugs honestly have no clue, and it's not fair to utilize the old standby of yelling whenever they make mistakes and act inappropriately. Instead, they need consistent and specific instruction on how you want them to act. "We pet the kitty nicely" and "We do not take toys from other children" are a couple of sentences I have burned into my frontal lobe.

It makes a world of difference to give toddlers specific coaching on how they're supposed to act. Pat phrases like, "Don't do that!" and "Stop that or else!" are vague and useless. They have no idea what you're talking about! Toddlers need to know precisely what it is you do and do not want.

If you're a mushy parent, this technique can be challenging. When you say something like, "We do not hit Mommy," your child could have the attitude, "Oh yeah? Well, I just did it." You can avoid this attitude if you *don't let her do it again*. Let the first time your daughter hits you be the last before she discovers some consequences. Hold her arm, look her in the eye, and tell her firmly "We do not hit Mommy" one more time. Remember the two rules of engagement? Say what you mean and do what you say. Draw the line there, and if she tries to hit you again, put your foot down and go through with your consequence. Bad attitudes only arise when children don't trust our word.

"Ah, Ah" (No more "No!")

I'm on a mission to try and eliminate use of the word "No!" (I can dream, can't I??). Sure, sometimes it's appropriate. But mercy alive, kids constantly copy us. If we stop modeling it so much, maybe they'll stop yelling it back so much. So let's try and replace it. Here are two choices to try:

Use a generic vocalization. Say something like "anh!" or a quick "ah, ah!" Just a 'no-no' type vocalization or sound without actually saying "no".

When your child reaches the age of about eighteen to twenty four months, and has a better comprehension of language, try using "We do not."

When you see behavior you do not like, gently take your child's hand or arm to get his attention, make him look you in the eye if you can, then use one of the two options. For older toddlers, you can say things like "We do not hit other children." "We do not run away from Mommy." "We do not play with our food." Keep it simple and direct. Don't drone on and on about why we don't do it. Just state the facts. And if they try to keep it up, move on to "If...then" (below).

In addition to using the phrase, "We do not", offer an alternative and tie it in with "We (do)" or "You may". Say something like, "We do not hit baby sister. You may give her a toy instead" or "We do not throw our books, we read them." Give toddlers something they MAY do instead of filling their ears with everything they may not. If your child is running into the wall with a push toy, tell her, "We do not run into the wall with toys. You may run it into the couch instead."

It's cool to stay away from negatives and focus on the positive/what you WANT to see. For a 16-month-old, a phrase like "Don't hit Mommy" translates into, "blah, blah, HIT MOMMY" and they'll turn around and sock you again - because that's all they heard! With one-year-olds, it works better to use your "anh!" vocalization or say, "No hitting. You may give a kiss instead." <u>Always offer the guidance of a positive redirection.</u>

"If...then..."

Let your child know the consequence of her actions in preparation for what will happen. When an undesired behavior creeps up, tell her "we do not..." about two times. If the behavior continues, go to the next step. Inform her, for example, "If you keep banging your plate, Mommy will take it away." Repeat this twice, max. No cooperation? *Go through* with what you say. Nine times out of ten, your child is keeping up with the behavior just to see what you'll do. Be prepared for a tantrum even though you've given plenty of warnings. Acting like the world's coming to an end when you follow through with your consequences is part of a toddler's duty. And by the way, don't give the darn plate back five seconds later. Take it away, and you are <u>done</u> with meal time. Being more interested in banging than eating means they aren't that hungry.

I'm always fascinated to see a child meltdown after being told exactly what will happen if they do not cooperate with a request. They act like they're being held down and forced to eat spinach when all you've done is tell them something as benign as "If you throw the book, I will take it away." I haven't met a kid yet who doesn't like to test his limits. Yet they often seem quite baffled when you actually go through with a promise. Take, for instance, the child used to running the show and consistently getting his own way. Oooooh, holy cow. Confusion registers like a slap in the face when you actually take away the toy being thrown or used to pummel another kid. They simply aren't used to adults actually doing what they say. Most often they initially bring down the roof with anger, but magically become more cooperative as time goes on. The change is downright startling!

Go through with your promise when you use an "If...then" statement. Children LIKE to know that you keep your word! It builds faith and confidence. Toddlers learn to stay calm because they know you *really will* give them their lunch in "just a minute", or you *really will* play with them as soon as you finish the dishes. Teach your child to trust you when you make a promise. They deserve honesty.

"It's for looking, not touching..."

Not long after I gave birth to my first child, I took her to work, showing her off to my fellow teachers and therapists. When one of the special needs kiddos, Andrew, tried to touch her, his teacher gently took his hand and said, "Babies are for looking, not touching". It was such a funny statement that I almost laughed – but gadzooks, it worked! That cutie pie Andrew didn't get upset or offer one word of protest. He simply pulled his hand back, looked up at his teacher, and said, "Okay." I took a vow right then and there to add that phrase to my repertoire!

When on a walk and your kids are tearing into a neighbor's flowers, tell them, "Flowers are for looking, not touching...they are very delicate." Glass balls on Christmas trees, pictures frames, and breakables all get this classification. It's a great little phrase and helps toddlers understand why we can't touch every tempting thing we see.

One tragic day our faithful washing machine had a major heart attack. My husband valiantly performed emergency surgery in an effort to save it. Sadly, the washing machine passed on to appliance heaven, and as a result of the failed operation, the motor sat on our kitchen table for a day. We never once told Poppy to stay away from it, but after her initial visual inspection, she promptly said to herself, "It's looking, not touching." She used the phrase all the time and had no problem instructing her little sister Mimi. Anytime Mimi went for the T.V. controls, cabinet contents, trash, or heaven help us all, picked up one of Poppy's shoes and threatened to snack on it, she got a desperate and resounding, "No, no, Mimi! It's looking, not touching!"

You can also vary this phrase a little and use it for different situations. Example: "Pens are for paper, not your face" or "Sockets are for plugs, not fingers." Some other good ones are: "Food is for eating, not playing" and "Soap is for washing, not eating." (Good grief, who can keep up with all this eat/don't eat business?) Apply it to whatever you want; it works in so many ways.

Now, there's a word of warning in using this phrase. Don't overdo it and make everything on the planet off limits. Whenever possible, get down to your child's level and let your toddler see the untouchables. They need to get some of the fascination out of their system, so encourage exploration. When possible, take two minutes out of your day and let your toddler handle an off-limits item. Have your kiddo turn the object over in their hands and feel the texture. Let them get a sense of the weight and delicate nature of the item. When finished, tell them it's time to put it back, and make sure to praise the success with being gentle.

"I need you to…" "I want you to…"

To eliminate guesswork, use the "I need" phrase to tell your child exactly what you want, or divert attention when Little Bit fitfully can't communicate what *she* wants. For example, if your child's upset because you put in the wrong DVD, get down on her level and tell her, "I need you to stop crying and tell Mommy which video you want to watch. I cannot understand when you cry." Or, if she wakes up howling

86

in the middle of the night, say something like, "I need you to calm down and tell Mommy what's wrong." After she tells you and requests a comfort item (like a cup of water), tell her "I'll get you some water, but I need you to lie down." (Again, this is contingent on the need being real, not an attention-getting routine...in which case your reply will be "It's not time for water. It's time for bed." *Right??!!*)

This instruction phrase sets up our **A** (in TAG) for success. Here we go again with telling your child exactly what you *want* to see, not what you don't. You don't actually have to say "I want you to," but it helps to keep your line of thought clear. Just what is it you want? Believe me, it's a different way of thinking and takes practice. I still catch myself and have to think about it instead of blurting out a negative. Here are some examples:

Instead of "stop fussing" say, "I want you to use a quiet voice."

Instead of "stop hitting" say, "I want you to keep your hands to yourself."

Instead of "cut it out" say, "Keep your bottom still while sitting at the table."

Instead of "don't run" say, "Walk slowly."

"Let's"

Using the word "let's" is a great way to increase desirable behavior and promote cooperation. For instance, instead of "Don't play with the plant" you can say, "Let's not play with the plant. Let's play with the car instead." This way, you are asking nicely and redirecting. Children are more apt to cooperate if you ask nicely and offer to help by saying, "Let's put this away now." You can also say things like, "Let's go change your diaper" or "Let's put on your shoes." Using "let's" indicates collaboration yet makes it clear you're the boss. Words are powerful, and "let's" is a respectful way of commanding cooperation. When you are kind and deferential, you teach your child respect.

Here are some examples of ways to use the catch phrases:

It's not time to play on the computer; it's time to eat breakfast. Thank you for listening.

Let's not play with the scissors.

Let's not chase the kitty.

Let's clean this up. Please help Mommy.

We do not sit on baby sister. We sit *next* to her. Thank you.

We do not throw blocks. You may stack them instead. (OR) Blocks are for stacking, not throwing.

We leave our socks on when it's cold outside.

We write on paper, not on the table.

We are out of eggs. You may have hot cereal for breakfast.

We do not need a whole box of crayons. You may have three.

Christmas trees are for looking, not touching. Good listening.

If you splash Mommy again, you will get out of the bathtub.

If you eat your chicken, you may have ice cream.

I need you to be quiet; your brother is sleeping.

I need you to read your books while Mommy is on the phone.

Terrific Transitions!

My sympathy strings get a good yank when I see a child throwing a fit at the end of a great party or when it's time to leave the park or weekly playdate. Totally the end of the world to a toddler having so much fun! Some kids are more flexible than others, and your child's personality greatly influences the ability to switch activities. Children who're spirited, active, detail-oriented, or obsessive about finishing projects/activities usually have more difficulty with transitions. But given the correct guidance from caregivers, they can learn to transition well.

I swear to the park gods, not two weekends ago, my husband and I saw a mother and father tell their two young boys it was time to leave. The first kid fired back, "No, losers!" Then the second popped out, "Yeah, no way, loser boozer!" I froze in morbid fascination. My husband's jaw dropped. Just...holy...are my ears working? Did those kids just freaking call their parents 'losers'??!! And did those parents just walk away and do nothing?! Well, knock me over with a feather, I do believe those kids are right – loser parents letting their kids be so disrespectful! Amen, brother. Looks like we need a little work on transitions, my friends!

There are some superb catch phrases you can use to avoid dragging a kicking, screeching kid away from the park or out the door of your neighbor's house. Believe me, I've been there and done that. The embarrassment justifies fainting. Making every pathetic excuse in the book, I once made a complete ass of myself to very polite neighbors before giving up and surrendering to fate. The screaming fit that was my child had to be peeled off the playhouse, slung over my shoulder, and oh-so-carefully navigated out the door. Who the hell expects to be wielding a thirty pound octopus grabbing onto every available wall fixture, door frame, and lock of hair?

Your ticket to terrific transitions lies in these straightforward words (which by the way, I failed to use in the above example): **"bye-bye", "all done" or "finished", "sleepy"** and **"one more time".** Simple as they sound, _as long as children are not hungry or tired_, these powerful words can work miracles. Start using these phrases as early as possible – seven or eight months old. Regularly spout utterances like, "Time to go bye-bye" and "We're all finished with the ice cream."

When you initially introduce these transition words, you may find that your child still gets upset. But he might use the phrases to comfort himself as he works through the disappointment. He may wail something along the lines of "ooooohhhh, all done!" while crying and jabbering on in unintelligible toddler lingo. All this is well and good, as he's learning how to deal with the difficult and upsetting emotions.

"Sleepy" is actually a transition my older daughter thought up, pairing it with the ending of an activity. During the summer of her second year, my husband would frequently take her to the park. Walking together, they would pass a creek bed and talk about the stars, moon, and frogs. She loved the sound of the frogs. Over time, summer turned to winter and the frogs stopped croaking. She wanted to know why. Chris (my husband) told her it was wintertime and too cold for them, so they went away. She paused a moment and said, "Oh, frogs asleep."

Since then, the park, the computer, dolls, her dear friend down the street, or anything else she wants to play with, "have to go sleepy" when it's time to transition. Even the sun goes sleepy when it's nighttime. Children love a simple reason why things have to stop or go away, and transitional phrases help them work through any disappointment.

Another great phrase is "one more time." When you need to leave the park, tell your child "one more time" on the slide or swing. The key to this is that you MUST go through with what you say. Do not utter the phrase "one more time" only to let your toddler go two or three more rounds on the equipment. That's not fair or honest (liar, liar, pants on fire!) and only reinforces that you do not mean what you say. When you use the phrase "one more time" or "one more" and go through with your promise, there may still be a few tears, but you will eventually find that cooperation is easier to come by. (And maybe, just maybe, your kid won't call you a 'loser'. How nice!)

Here are more examples of ways to use the transitional phrases:

We're all finished at the park. Time to go home now. Say "bye-bye" to the park!

We can't go to the park now – it's sleepy.

The crackers are all gone; say "bye-bye" to the crackers!

Katie can't play right now – she's sleepy.

When to Drop the Baby Talk: Toddlers really do understand much more than they let on. Once in a while you'll even run into one who can discuss the current presidential race or abstract enough to ask, "Do people live on Mars, Mommy?" So herein lies the question of when to increase the complexity of your language and drop the very basic baby talk. Obviously, kids acquire language at varying speeds. Telling a language efficient three-year-old that the park has to go sleepy may be confounding, if not blatantly lunatic. Your smarty-pants could easily pipe back, "Parks don't sleep! Parks aren't even alive! Look it up on the 'puter, Momma."

At what point you decide to drop the short, concise phrases and address your toddler with the "let's have a little discussion" approach is entirely up to you. As a general guideline, one and two-year-olds benefit the most from the simple power phrases and transitional statements. Three-year-olds understand a more complex speech like, "You're having too many accidents in your pants. We are now going to sit on the potty every hour, whether you think you need to go or not. That's the new rule, so get used to it."

As a speech therapist, I'm obligated to remind you that your three-year-old does not necessarily have to be communicating well enough to drive you crazy with incessant questions like "Do birds' feathers help them fly?" "What causes thunder?" "How was the Earth made?" If it works to keep your language simple, then by all means, do so. Your Mommy instincts will tell you when your child understands more than he's letting on. Besides, even if your two-year-old *does* understand that you don't tell crackers bye-bye, and parks don't go to sleep, making your statements a little more complex doesn't guarantee cooperation. Activity transitions and life rules are abstract and difficult concepts. Toddlers will have tantrums and angry fits, regardless of their language skills. Your little scholar may have a command of English, but he doesn't yet have a command of life.

Praise

Praise those little critters for positive behavior, and be specific. When sipping juice instead of slinging it, praise them! If they put their hat on straight (oh, heck...even if it's crooked), praise them! If they come the first time you call them for lunch, let you wipe snot off their nose, sit still while you put on their socks, or let you brush their hair, praise them! "Oh, I like the way you're sipping your juice so nicely; You did such a great job putting on your hat; Thank you for listening when I called you for lunch; Good job letting Mommy wipe your nose; Thank you so much for keeping your feet still while Mommy put your socks on; I just love the way you're sitting quietly so Mommy can comb your beautiful hair." Specifically letting your child know what pleases you motivates him to keep up the great behavior.

Feel free to express your pleasure with rewards (although keep the tangibles in moderation) and **always** give verbal praise with lots of hugs and kisses. There's no replacement for verbal approval and acts of love. Kids can't get enough. They could care less about the new book you brought home if it means they have to read it alone. Toddlers are attention-craving creatures. Time and attention is IT. New 'things' aren't needed to make them happy. Simple activities like shelling pecans together or coloring in a ratty coloring book make them pleased as punch.

Overdoing Praise: Having bopped you on the head with making sure you praise for everything, I'm going to back up a bit and give you a small warning. Be mindful that it's possible to *over* praise. If you jump up and down dancing the Can-Can every time your child pushes down the Velcro on his shoe, he'll wonder where your mind went. It's okay to praise, just don't hound him with wild and ecstatic applause if he isn't particularly interested, or the behavior or task isn't exactly noteworthy. If you go overboard with exaltation, the meaning fizzles. *And* they'll grow up expecting "atta boy!" for simply showing up for high school classes or the after school job. Hello! We don't want that!

Praise when you find yourself genuinely happy your toddler did a good job, and stay away from nonspecific, repetitive phrases like "good job", "good boy", and "that's so nice!" In and of themselves, these phrases are not pointless and insincere, but if you use them when your child is just sitting still and trying to figure out a puzzle, he'll be confused – because he hasn't *done* anything. Be more detailed by saying "You're doing a great job fitting those pieces into the puzzle" or "That was nice of you to kiss baby brother." And learn to expect a certain amount of good behavior. There's nothing wrong with letting your toddler know when you're pleased with cooperation, but if you bombard him with praise all day long, it loses the reward quality and becomes an expectation instead of genuine guidance.

Teaching Patience

Aside from the relentless nature of toddler needs, I'd say their tempers are the biggest exasperation for Mommies. Bad humor and quick hot buttons occasionally grind us into microbes. If a puzzle piece won't fit, they throw it. If they can't squeeze themselves under the bed, by golly, heads are gonna roll. If dress-up beads get stuck around our darling's neck, she'll practically choke herself with rage getting them off.

Toddlers are a walking definition of aggravation, and from their vantage point, who could blame them? The list is endless: They're too short to catch all the action adults get to see. Their bottom half is so uncoordinated that they constantly trip, yielding bonked heads and scraped knees. Adults insist they eat disgusting green vegetables for dinner instead of ice cream. Other pint-sized little monsters threaten their life and steal their toys. The pet turtle refuses to cuddle. Mommies go ape over a ludicrous article of clothing called "underwear" and badger the poor tot to sit on the toilet for no conceivably good reason. Cell phones are off limits, and Mommy locks up all the knives. More often than not, just when things get interesting, all hell breaks loose and they get tossed into a time-out. If I were a toddler, I'd be on a permanent protest of life's unfairness too.

Asking an irritable toddler to be patient is like asking a cat to bark. Patience is hard enough to practice as an adult. Toddlers can't even pull a shirt over their head without losing all sense of tolerance and howling, "Aarrrrrggghhh! I stuck! I stuck!" How on earth are they supposed to wait for a tuna fish sandwich when plummeting blood sugar rules out all sense of control? These sweet little buggers live in the here and now, and if it's not now, it's not ever.

Keeping the limited knowledge of time in mind, teach your toddler to trust you by going through with your promises. If you need your little one to be patient while you make her lunch, tell her. Don't get side tracked into a phone conversation or run outside to give the skunky dog a quick bath. If you say you're going to make lunch 'in a minute', make sure you're slicing oranges once that sixty seconds is up. Toddlers will also be more patient if they can help. Set up a chair for your sweet pea and let her take the plastic off cheese slices or pour a can of soup into a pot.

If frustration is the issue rather than time, do your best not to intervene until you see steam coming out of your little teapot. Toddlers need to learn how to problem solve on their own. If you always come to the rescue within two seconds of the first grunt of anger, they cannot learn how to deal with obstacles and aggravation. Plus, kids need their parents to back off a bit and not be so overbearing. Don't hover over your children and play with them 24/7; they need an occasional break from you. They deserve their own space and time to figure things out. It increases independence and creates alone time for you as well.

When you see the tension and anger building up and explosion is imminent, provide some **prompts**. Remember, the most effective prompt is physical, but it also requires the most hands-on work from you. Keep your voice very calm - even overly calm - and walk them through the task, such as opening a bucket of Lego's. Provide encouragement by saying, "Let's be patient. Here, Mommy will help you." Put his hand on the box and help him open it. You might even put the lid back on the box, setting it up for your child to try again. Once the box is opened, congratulate your child and remind her that being patient helps solve problems.

To minimize frustration, toddlers need tasks that are challenging but not too tricky. With too difficult an undertaking, many toddlers will walk away, but others go for it with gusto, getting exceedingly discouraged and angry. That's when tinker toys turn into rockets and threaten to put your eye out. Keep toys age appropriate to the best of your ability.

Listen, I believe your assertion that your little genius is the smartest guy in his preschool class, but he still doesn't have the dexterity to master the game of Operation. He's more likely to buzz his way into a major tantrum and give you a major headache.

Being a Patient Mommy

I wish attaining fortitude and serenity were as simple as a pep talk, but alas, I live in the real world. If the Mommies of toddlers had the magic potion in a bottle, we'd all be addicted. Too many nights I fall into bed and berate myself for a shortage of tolerance throughout the day. The triggering and offensive event seems so much more exasperating and dramatic in real time. It sucks when you look back on losing your temper because your child hurled the ketchup covered chicken nuggets across the kitchen. Retrospectively, the crime just doesn't seem all that bad. After all, nobody was hurt, ketchup is a removable stain (sometimes), and the dog ended up one happy camper.

One night my daughter was desperately bawling to Daddy, "Hebeju, hebeju!" but he just couldn't understand what she wanted. The minutes ticked on, the wailing got worse, but the sentence (do you call that a sentence?) was the same…"Hebeju, hebeju!" Exhausted after an incredibly busy day, he could have just stuck her in bed and let her deal with it. Instead, my husband spent ten minutes going through our entire kitchen pantry trying to figure out what she was trying to communicate.

Maintaining his calm demeanor, he finally told her to point out what she wanted. She went straight to the juicer and said it again, "Hebeju." I heard Daddy say, "*Ooooh!* You want to help make juice?" Her cries turned to relief mixed with laughter as she repeated the phrase. She'd been helping Daddy make fresh juice every night with our electric juicer, and she was ready for the ritual again. Had he not exercised great patience, she would have been put to bed heartbroken over something so easy to fix. All she wanted was to keep up with the routine Daddy had established.

When your toddler shreds the deed to your house or makes a marker mural out of baby brother, and you're two seconds from morphing into a pit bull, dig deep down into your reserves of patience. Mommies are usually the last stop when toddlers look for approval, love, and help. When you miss the chance to be tender and kind with your child, you know as well as I, the regrets and remorse stink!

Don't Pull a Sister Phyllis: For my generation, growing up in Catholic schools insured having a nun for a teacher at least one year of your academic career. The fate of fifth grade had me placed in the class of a nun who was, I swear to habaneros, mean as a snake. In all fairness, I must say she was the only nasty nun I ever ran into, but why on God's green Earth she was placed working with children, I will never fathom. Sister Phyllis was a woman whose pot was always boiling and ready to blow. If you were unfortunate enough to be a scatterbrain like me, you'd catch her wrath lightening quick. Once making the inexcusable mistake of handing in the math homework from page 75 instead of 76, and being all of eleven years old, I was sure I'd never see the light of another day. She'd close her eyes, clench her teeth, and slowly count to ten. When she finally opened those dark, raging slits of fury, boom! You'd see it. Your life flashing before you. Goner! Say your prayers, Rabbit!

By sheer force of nature, children push us to our outer most limits of patience. If you find yourself about to pull a Sister Phyllis, put your child someplace safe, and *walk away*. Take a five-minute break, get a glass of iced tea, do some deep breathing, or go bruise your toes on the couch. Do whatever's necessary to keep your calm and not take out inferno-anger on your kids.

Life with Toddlers

Everybody is allowed a bad day every now and then, but in the midst of your day from hell, try to remember your child's age. They're just learning what makes the world go round. It isn't their intention to drive us batty. They just want to know what'll happen if they shake chocolate milk onto your four thousand dollar Karastan rug or how long they'll need to howl before you give them an Oreo. It's not personal - just the business of being a toddler.

Chapter Four Review: What Did We Learn?

Six ways to set up an environment of trust, security, and control:

1. Start with Respect

2. No Yelling

3. Model Desirable Behaviors

4. Provide Structure and Routine

5. Repetition of Rules

6. The Two Rules of Engagement

Eight **Power Phrases** to increase cooperation.

Five Phrases to help with Transitions.

When to drop the Baby Talk.

The importance of praise (don't over-do it!).

Teaching toddlers patience, and being the patient Mommy.

Chapter Five: How to Handle Everyday Challenges

I'd love to tell you to duck and run when the going gets rough. In fact, you know what? I will. Run like the wind! Go, go, go! Right behind ya, baby!

Okay, seriously. The harsh reality is that the going will get rough almost everyday, and if it doesn't, count your blessings. Can we even begin to recall how many times we feel like whimpering and crawling back under the covers of our toasty bed? Or how many times we've called our husbands or friends, venting in hysteria, only to glance at the clock and see that lunch was still a dreadfully long two hours away?

Knowing When to Listen, Distract, or Put a Foot Down

Being a fantastic Mommy definitely has its mental dilemmas. For example, how on earth do we know what strategies to implement and when? Let's say sixteen-month-old Ralphie is whining because he's not allowed to eat the dishwashing crystals. We've got three choices: listen to his complaint, distract him from misery, or put our foot down and insist he learns to stay away from the countless toxins we use to clean our home. The hard part is figuring out *when* to listen, distract, or put our foot down. We Mommies tend to second-guess ourselves right into therapy.

Listening: One of the most valuable lessons in child rearing is to listen to kids when they're upset. Many Mommies try to distract their toddlers when the tantrums start, but this only crams the child's emotion back in like stuffing a genie into a bottle. I see these same kids throw fits and act out more than any others. Distraction definitely has a place in the life of a toddler, but consistently using it to ward off tantrums sounds more like a bribe to me.

When your child gets upset for any reason other than hunger or fatigue, *let her go through the emotions!* Let her cry sometimes and get the frustrations out instead of immediately trying to distract her. Get down to her level, offer a hug, then look her in the eye and listen to the gobbledygook of toddler talk. Say something understanding; "Really? You must feel awful." If you know exactly what your child's upset about, you can also validate her feelings by saying something like, "I know you're very upset because Mommy turned off your video. I'm sure that makes you feel sad." When you validate the trampled feelings of your little one, it puts a label on the emotion and lets your child know that you hear and understand the reason for the tears.

Distracting: Redirection is good for things like repeatedly touching a no-no, intense screaming due to frustration (i.e., they can't get a toy into a container and refuse to give up), or yelling in the car. For example, when screeching in the confines of an automobile, softly sing a song and try to get them engaged. Or crank up some classical music and open up the windows. (And yes, we're all human, so when this doesn't work, pull over, turn around, and glare the fear of God into them.) However, when it comes to tantrums, for the most part I do not recommend distraction unless the wailing is a direct result of hunger or fatigue. If toddlers are fed, rested, and truly upset about one of life's many disenchantments, they need to learn how to deal with disappointment, sadness, frustration, and anger.

Many children lack this skill and it's evident in the amount of crying they do. Mommies of these kids tend to whip out the coolest things from their purse, or pull the first thing they find off a store shelf and wave it around hypnotically. Rather amazing, really, the talent these Mommies have for coming up with new and interesting things to divert the attention of the little time bomb. (Remember Evelyn from the baseball movie, "A League of Their Own"? Whip out the chocolate! Shut that kid up!) But habitually using distraction to ward off tantrums will eventually come back to bite you. You're just trying to avoid the emotional outburst, but toddlers are too smart. They'll quickly figure out your ruse and refuse to be fooled.

Distraction is appropriate after you've given sympathy to the damaged ego and let your precious know that you hear and understand the cries of injustice. If your child cannot seem to regain composure after one to three minutes of wailing, and you're frantic to hold on to what's left of your sanity, feel no guilt in breaking out the juice and other culinary Band-Aids. Be my guest and distract away. Fish crackers or cookies work wonders when kids get into a scuffle, can't get their socks on, or fall and scrape their knees. Suggesting a treat is nothing less than miraculous whenever feelings are battered, tempers flare, and hearts break.

This is also a great tool if you desperately need your toddler to cooperate. No one will die if you let your little one play with your phone when you're late for a doctor's appointment and she's refusing to put her shoes on. Whatever gets the task accomplished quickly is sometimes the best avenue. I know it's hard and the inevitable kink will occur, but plan ahead as much as possible, giving yourself enough time to get ready; you'll cut down on the lack of cooperation. Remember, the little psychics forever sense haste and choose that time to decide, "I do it byself!"

Distracting with Television: Tons of toddler experts and parents abhor the idea of using the boob tube as a babysitter. They are right. However - I must take a moment to extol the virtues of limited television. Now hold on, Mommy! Don't faint with horror just yet! This outlandish opinion isn't quite as disgraceful as it sounds upfront.

Having raised two toddlers and fully engaged with #3, I refrain from freaking out over the issue of *selective* T.V., because I happen to be a rather realistic gal. I'm well aware that sticking a toddler in front of the television turns them into a slack-jawed zombie. I'm also well aware that I sometimes get so overloaded with toddler turmoil that I need the peace and quiet more than I need to feel guilty for letting my kids watch thirty minutes of a charming educational video.

The early evening crank monster has a tendency to possess young children without any consideration for whether or not you're having a bad day. Cramps, a missed shower or strep throat are of no consequence to end-of-day toddlers. My own little gerbils would consistently scurry around the house and try to attack each other if I didn't keep them fed, separated, and occupied.

There are times when I'm feverish and miserable, or so fed up that "no" (or several variations on that theme), are the only utterances out of my crabby mouth. When my poor children get nothing but exasperated attention from me, I'm fairly certain the positive alternative is to separate the little pixies from my grumpy attitude. If television is the only thing (or okay, the easiest thing) that'll dissolve the angry glue holding us together, so be it.

Sure, I could set them up with some paint or blocks, and cheerfully tell them to play nicely so I can double over on the couch for ten minutes, frantically wash my face and douse myself with powder, or go and gargle with hot salt water. But the reason I forego using activities as a distraction when the entire family is circling the drain is because the activity materials end up being used as props in a theatrical production starring my unruly children. Unfailingly, the paint winds up splattered all over my kitchen, and the blocks are labeled "Exhibit A" from a crime scene in which the perpetrator dumps the entire container of wooden squares on the victims head.

Any Mommy currently taming wild critters will tell you there are times when you simply need a break. I'm forever convinced that thirty minutes of selective T.V., here and there, will not bestow children with permanent brain damage or drop their I.Q.'s enough to warrant repeating preschool. There are plenty of fabulous toddler videos pairing classical music with creative imagery of seasons, numbers, letters, animals, shapes, and a myriad of other fascinating toddler topics. Little people go nuts over them. Plus, I have yet to find anything wrong with Barney (other than being extremely irritating), Dora, and Blues Clues.

Obviously, these shows don't replace the value and importance of actually playing and being active, but it's a darn nice option of distraction when Mommy's about to reach cerebral meltdown. If anyone gets on your tail about letting your kids watch a little supervised and selective T.V., tell them to stuff it. Otherwise, they're more than welcome to come and take over. I'm thinking, "Have at it, you unsympathetic nag!"

When to Plant Your Foot: After you've listened to your child's trauma and demonstrated understanding, do not give in to any protests. Sure, it stinks when Mommy insists the pet snake not be swung around like a lasso, but that's life, kiddo. After you've been sympathetic to the emotional distress, *put your foot down*. Once your little zookeeper gets out of control and starts throwing a colossal fit, it won't help to listen, distract, or offer comfort. Leave him alone and let him recompose.

Planting your foot is also needed when your child so much as *begins* to be demanding. Even if little Troy isn't in full battle gear yet, you can be sure that demanding behavior means he's gearing up for tantrum combat. Lending your ear when he's insistent and overbearing will serve no purpose but to make him think you can be manipulated. Listening and being sympathetic will not make Troy any less demanding. What *will* make him less demanding is to give a calm, but resolute, "no" to his bossy mandate. You can certainly "mirror" or repeat his concern to let him know that you did indeed hear what he said – "I understand you want to go outside now, but it's not time to go outside. It's time to eat." After that, lay down the law and stand your ground.

If little Troy decides to commence with Armageddon, let him go through the emotions. Walk away or pick him up and deposit him in another room away from you, and go back to what you were doing. Give him some time to calm down while you try to figure out the problem. Is he hungry and tired? If so, meet those needs. First, do your best to get him to eat. Don't go hog wild and set out five different entrees, but offer what you've prepared and tell him he'll feel better if he eats. If he refuses and continues to tantrum, put the little guy to bed. Don't follow him around in an attempt to shove two more bites down his throat or try every trick in the book so he'll consume one more ounce of sandwich. If you sit him at the table and he chooses not to eat, respect his decision. He won't starve, and his need for sleep may be greater than food.

Toys

When the going gets rough, toys are often a good place to implement some positive change. Some toddlers need the playroom scaled down. The more demanding the child, the more limits are needed. If your child has a plethora of toys, yet still seems whiny, irritable, difficult, and cannot seem to entertain herself well, start by boxing up half (or more) of her toys. This gives your child a much-needed break from the task of having to choose from so many items to play with.

When deciding which toys to put away and which to leave out, opt for boxing up the high-tech toys and leaving the old fashioned and classic items in the toy bin. There are certain playthings kids consistently entertain themselves with day after day. Simple items like puzzles, blocks, dolls, crayons, stuffed animals, baskets, cars, books, balls, shape sorters, and of course, the animal sounds farm are usually highly prized items. The anxiety of putting away the expensive and oh-so-cute (but over-stimulating) toys may have you thinking twice, but relax. The anxiety is yours, not your kid's. Take a chill pill and give the kid a break from the overload. You can get the dadgum toys back out later. Plus, if push came to shove and you were to get rid of 80% of the lot, I bet your kid wouldn't miss a beat.

Explanations…and Balance

When it comes to explaining why we don't do X, Y, or Z, here's a rule you can live by and feel good about:

Once emotions start to stir, you do not owe your child an explanation.

Period. End of story. If the child is out of control, there is no need to explain anything. She's beyond reckoning. Explanations are absolutely appropriate – and sometimes extremely helpful – but only when you're both calm and in control. When peacefully playing together and your toddler gets a bit rough with the dog, you can say, "We do not hit doggie. It hurts." Or, you can provide instruction and alternatives: "We do not hit the dog. We pet gently." Explanations are acceptable during relaxed interactions. But once emotions begin to stir from either of you, turn off the explanation button.

My friend Amy uses an approach to raising her child that we call "the explanation method", which she came up with on her own. Her method consists of explaining - well, *everything*. (Makes me dizzy. Seriously.) You give reasons 'why' anytime they come up. "We don't pull on cabinet doors honey; they could break off." "You need to get dressed quickly or we'll be late for school, and then you'll miss morning calendar." "Please eat over the table or you'll get crumbs all over the floor." There's no simple "put the book away." It's always "put the book away *because…*"

Amy's theory is that when a child understands "why" they'll be more likely to cooperate. I believe it's true – especially with certain personalities. As long as a child isn't out of control, explaining does seem to increase cooperation, especially as the child matures. For some reason (who knows what) they seem to appreciate knowing why they can't do such-in-such or why you're making such a fuss over getting out the door quickly. For Amy, this method is a way of life, not something you implement only when you feel like it or remember. Taken as a whole, it raises the child with respect as a family member while teaching respect for others and appropriate actions.

And now...the catch. (You just knew I'd say that, didn't you?) This method works, to be sure; I've tried it myself. With good consistency, limits, and structure already in place, this method ties it all together. However, as with all things in life, there's a true hickey to this works-so-well-method. The hitch is this: time. This method is so darn time consuming that you need some serious discipline and motivation to keep it up. Amy's an über-mom, giving her daughter 100% of her time at *all* times. And guess what that means? Amy is exhausted. All the time. She moans and groans about needing a break ten times more than me and she only has *one* kid; but a darn happy one. Lily's a true peach – cooperative, smart, and caring. Is it innate, or because Amy spends so much time letting Lily's character develop in the best way possible? Who knows? But it's a great example of what could be if you put forth the effort.

Which brings us to balance. Everything in life is about balance. The balancing act of raising toddlers is flooded with guilt, happiness, confusion, and of course, exhaustion. There's a balance to providing explanations to our kids. If you're able to give constant explanations, more power to you. Personally, I think the incessant and relentless nature of their needs puts this method on the difficult side, but it is possible. Try it. Just make sure to balance it. *Don't* offer explanations once emotions stir on the negative or your child gets out of control. Your requests are what they are, and kids can simply learn to live with it.

"I'm Sorry, But We Don't Play With That, Okay?"

Oh, Mommy. How do I put this delicately? Forget it, I can't. DON'T APOLOGIZE FOR YOUR RULES! And don't tell your toddler to do something, then turn around and ask him if it's okay. Example: A Mommy in the mall earnestly tells her little track stars, "Stop running, okay?!" I mean, are you *kidding* me? Do you think her kids are actually going to agree with the ridiculous request? Running in the mall is fun, and if you ask me to stop then give me the option to agree or not...I'm thinking, "NOT!"

There is no way you'll get the respect you deserve if you apologize for your rules and give your kids the option to disagree with what you say. "I'm sorry, but it's not time to go to gym class" and "I'm sorry but you can't have candy for dinner, okay?" are sentences to be stricken from your Mommy-to-toddler vocabulary. Just get rid of the words "sorry" and "okay". I know you're sympathetic when boo-boo-face doesn't understand why he can't have the box of Raid Roach Kill or why he can't just hop in the car and go to his favorite tumbling class, but it's not your fault! There's no need to apologize or add "okay?" to the end of your sentences.

If you feel strongly about letting your child know you are equally heartbroken, then validate his feelings. Say something like "I know you're upset because you can't have Daddy's hammer. You want to play with it and Mommy won't let you. This must make you very sad." Let him know you're listening and understand his trauma. Just don't plead with him to stop breaking all your windows and apologize when you have to wrench the weapon out of his iron grip.

Some people say, "I'm sorry you feel that way", but this phrase makes me think someone is disappointed in their child's feelings. Look, people can feel the way they feel, and if you tell them otherwise, it promotes a sense of insecurity. Besides, (prepare for another humble opinion) the phrase is just lame. When someone tells you 'I'm sorry you feel that way'...what the hell is that supposed to mean? They aren't sorry. Sounds more like a passive aggressive way to say, 'you're an idiot and you're wrong.' We don't want to do that to our kids. Validation is certainly fine; "I understand you feel X, Y, and Z. I hear you." Beyond that, there's no real reason to comment on how *you* feel about how *they* feel.

The Appropriate "I'm Sorry": We all know Mommy and Daddy are the big people on the campus of life, but that's no reason to bully your children. This may be very difficult to hear, Mommy, but we're not always right. I recall with shame an incident when my daughter was playing with a bar of soap in the bathtub. Confiscating the soap when the bath was over, I snatched it out of her hand too quickly, and it fell to the floor, making her upset. And you know what? I almost didn't apologize. Why, I can't say. Pride, ego, stupidity - whatever it was almost kept me from doing what was right, even though I truly felt bad and didn't mean to grab the soap in such an abrupt manner. To this day, I'm so glad I got over myself, giving her a hug and telling her I was sorry.

If you make a mistake and your child gets upset, apologize! Appropriate apologies convey your care and concern about how you treat your family. Acts of contrition model fairness and accountability. Apologizing is completely dignified and lets your toddler know that everyone makes mistakes. Society must play a big part in making people feel like mistakes are not okay because most people seem to run like the blazes from admitting fault. Don't give in to this line of thinking. Apologize to your child when you're wrong. When you show him you care, he'll reciprocate with love and respect.

Now to the other extreme – sappy parenting. Here's the scenario: Our kid gets the wrong color Jell-O, so he throws the entire bowl on the floor, shattering the dish. He promptly gets yelled at and thrown into time-out. Five minutes of wailing later, what do we parents do? We go to our child, wracked with guilt, and offer up slobbering apologies, hugs, and another bowl of Jell-O. Excuse me, but....*aaaaahhhh!* What are we thinking?! We can't DO that if we're to teach our children respect! Offering apologies when we're clearly in the wrong is one thing. But offering rewards because we feel guilty when our *child* was clearly in the wrong is just plain screwy. Again, find that balance. Apologize when you're wrong, but do not reward undesirable behavior.

The Nitty Gritty on Sharing & Stealing

Before we go any further, let's get something out in the open. SHARING IS NOT NATURAL. Okay? I've said it. Sharing is not natural for mature people, much less our egocentric young. Really, how many of you don't mind lending your corvette to your sister every other day? What about merrily shacking up your husband's best friend until he finds a job? Any of you pregnant Mommies mind sharing your food? Maybe you're a better person, but when I'm pregnant, anyone so much as glancing at my hamburger is in for hell. Honestly, we don't share because we *want* to. We share because we should. From a very young age, we've been taught to share with others. We don't want to, but we do.

Toddlers are uncivilized versions of adults. They have not yet learned how to grit their teeth and smile while handing over a prized possession. When playing with an object or toy, some toddlers are very agreeable to handing it over or giving it up when asked. If not, they can learn this skill.

But we really aren't talking about sharing in the true sense of "this is mine and you can have some." What we're really talking about here is **_not stealing_**. Toddlers have no idea, nor do they give a horse's patoot, that it's uncouth to screech "Mine!" and forcefully seize any desired object from any person. Operating on raw emotion, toddlers are expected to act vehemently possessive because they have total freedom from guilt or conscience.

At some point, we have to teach the undomesticated little darlings some manners. I completely concede that sharing is not natural for the clueless little sweeties. But part of the life of a toddler is learning to temper your emotions and play nice with the other kiddies. Those are the rules, and there's no getting around these life lessons.

The best time to start teaching our toddlers how to interact with other civilized human beings is NOW. The longer we wait, the longer our children go along in life thinking they rule the roost. I nearly put a choke hold on a four-year-old recently who decided he was thirsty and literally tried to snatch my daughter's drink right out of her hand – *as* she was drinking. *What...what??* Where the heck were the manners? And for that matter, where the hell was the parent? This was a birthday party, for heaven's sake. Letting your offensive kid run wild at a party and expecting other Mommies to sweep up the mess is really dropping the ball, girl! Grrr!

Don't wait until your toddler's old enough to understand the concept of sharing (not stealing) before you introduce the need. You'd be waiting for the cows to come home, and besides, it bursts too big a bubble. Speaking from a purely logistical standpoint, it would also be a monster of a battle. If our little dumplings have been able to grab and yell their way through the first three or four years of life, it'd be a stand up fight convincing them the need to change. The longer you wait to introduce the life rule of sharing, the harder it'll be on everyone, especially your child.

The "Mine!" Complex

The "Mine!" complex is the antithesis of sharing. This complex is the extreme version of "I want it, I want it now, I'm going to take it, and you're going to deal with it." The rather unkind characteristics include excessive yelling of "Mine!" or "No!" and/or forcefully grabbing objects from innocuous hands.

The reason behind this aggressive complex starts out innocently enough. When first learning language, there's a process of figuring out what works. Children don't understand the inappropriate nature of grabbing desired objects, grunting, crying, and yelling, but they sure understand the quick results.

Toddlers can learn by example to moderate their abrupt approach and still get the same results. As a good modeling Mommy, we teach them to say something much more socially acceptable like, "I want to play with that" instead of, "MINE!" So when a toddler first starts to demonstrate the "Mine!" complex, jump on it. Model the correct response. If the ploy for possession hasn't become a habit, and your harmless cutie is still just getting the hang of language, there's no need to make a big deal about it. You can calmly tell your child, "When we want a toy, we say 'I want to play with that.'" And okay, maybe that's a bit wordy for a one-year-old – but even teaching a simple, "please" gets the point across.

As your child gets older, stronger, more mobile, and less inhibited, frankly, it's just too darn easy to snatch whatever they want whenever they want it. The quickest way to get the job done is to grab and go. Most toddlers will have an innate desire to possess every object in visual range. We just have to guide our children and demonstrate the sharing rules.

If your little one has carried the possessiveness too far and other kids start scrambling every time they see your child, then wake up. A few time-outs are needed. Whenever your child takes a toy from someone, TAG it quick. Why did she do it? When it's truly only because she wanted the toy, gently tell her that we do not take toys from other children and make her return the object. Be kind but firm, and if she throws a fit, put her in time-out. Giving no attention to the tantrum decreases the likelihood of recurrence.

You never really outgrow the need to have your own possessions or want what others have. I know a woman who for twelve long years has refused to share her most cherished cookie recipe with anyone, let alone me. Knowing her daughter for over twenty years allows no advantage – for the love of sugar, I was in SECOND GRADE with this girl! Her mom's frosted delights really are the best things I've ever tasted, but this woman acts as though someone will be stricken dead (or worse, profit from the sale) if she shares the recipe. I'm perpetually dumbfounded over the possessiveness. It's not as if the woman is willing to patent the secret ingredients and sell it; if she did, I'd be first in line to buy. She just refuses to share. It's absolutely crazy, selfish, and downright silly – which I'm not afraid to say since there's no hope of ever getting that recipe! Given this, my point is reiterated. First of all, it's her recipe. Second, I want it.

Isn't "Mine" Fine? They'll Outgrow it, Right? Occasionally, a child will develop the "Mine!" complex in the extreme form. When overwhelmed with the behavior, a Mommy might desperately cling to any advice that assures her child will outgrow the aggressiveness. This is sadly misleading. Yes, toddlers are perfectly predictable in their nature to yell and take toys from other children. All of our kids do it. And they'll still occasionally grab and shriek at each other despite our desperate attempts to guide them on decreasing the ferocious fights over toys. BUT, this does not mean that extreme possessiveness and consistent aggressive behavior is acceptable.

Constant badgering is disrespectful to other children and their Mommies. If your child grabs a toy from another little kid, be gentle, but let her know it's not tolerable. TAG it to figure out what's

114

reinforcing the behavior. Hate to say it, girly, but it's probably you. So stop! When you don't insist your toddler refrain from snatching, it's blatantly rude to the injured party and his (or her) Mommy. And good gravy, my friend, this creates an outright social minefield.

Being Objective: When looking at possessive behavior, be objective. It's perfectly okay for a child to want to hide his favorite baseball and bat from the twenty scavengers you've invited over for his third birthday party. But if the little guy's screaming "MINE!" and "NO!" while taking 90% of the toys away from 100% of the guests, then something is off.

Yes, spats will happen. Kids will grab and yell, even *with* needs being met - and if siblings are around, sheesh. Headache-ville. Just keep an eye on the frequency. Aggressive possessiveness should not be to such an extreme that other Mommies and kids are constantly ticked.

Be honest and objective. How often is your little precious yanking toys and demanding the enemy retreat? Is it a habit? Stop making excuses and address it, girl! Breaking up brawls is a must-do is when your child is the instigator (hard to imagine, but it does happen).

Mommy Has to Play Nice, Too: We need to play nice with other Mommies and children because it models respect. Feeling it's my professional duty, I must request your assistance as a fellow Mommy of future world leaders and peacemakers. No matter how you feel about it, if you happen to see your perfect pumpkin initiate an aggression (yell, push, bite, or unjustly take a toy from someone else's child), then I beg you to step in – as a matter of simple consideration for other adults and children.

I can't tell you how many times I witness an atrocious act or have an irked friend report one to me – and the Mommy of the offender does nothing. That goes against our Mommy Code of Ethics, ladies! If you see it happen or it's clear your kid was in the wrong, troubling as it is, you own it. Nothing gets you kicked out of the Girlfriend Club quicker than ignoring or being oblivious.

When you see your child swipe a toy from unsuspecting hands, take the toy from your child and tell them, "Max was playing with the ball. We do not take toys from other children." Give the toy back to the victim of the robbery, and tell them you're sorry. If your child is old enough, make them apologize as well.

A matter that bears stressing: _it does not matter if the victim is not crying or upset because the toy has been taken away._ Deal with your child's snatching whether the injured party is wailing uncontrollably or not. Some Mommies find it incredibly offensive when other Mommies don't address issues. So what if the victim didn't meltdown when her Barbie's head was ripped off during the mugging attempt? That was still horribly rude!

As the Mommy of a toddler, and possibly a couple of other critters, it'll be virtually impossible to catch all your child's negative actions towards other kids. Since most of us see only a small fraction of our child's dire deeds, it's important to act on the ones we do observe. For the most part, Mommies of victims are very gracious and will generously forgive or overlook a couple of spats initiated by another child. However, if the aggressive behavior becomes a habit, and the initiator's Mommy refuses to acknowledge what she sees, she may find her child's playmates suddenly and permanently too busy to get together. Yowza! That hurts!

Chapter Five Review: What Did We Learn?

When to Listen, Distract, or Put a Foot Down.

Decreasing the stimulation/overload from toys.

The art of explanations.

"I'm Sorry" and "okay" are no-no's!

The appropriate "I'm sorry."

How to stop "stealing" and the "Mine!" Complex.

Be objective when looking at your child's behavior!

Be respectful of other Mommies and their toddlers.

Chapter Six: Aggressors and Co-Conspirators

Brace yourself Mommy; at some point, it will happen. You cannot get along in this life without your child being bopped, punched, pushed, pulled, grabbed, thieved, whacked, kicked, or otherwise gravely threatened by another child. What do you do when it happens? Well, you have the permission of all the Poker Mommies of the world to cry your eyes out right along with your child. We've all been there and know a good cry works wonders.

The situations are so predictable. You get together with another kid and Mommy, and the playmate consistently snatches away your child's toys. Your little angel isn't too upset about the robberies, so there's no need to make a fuss, right? Anxiety creeps in, but the matter still goes without any bellows of protest. And hey, we're all big people. We know there's a certain amount of imposition a child needs to learn to deal with, as you cannot protect them all the time. Live-and-learn, that's our philosophy! So we make our child deal.

Well, holy moly if the poor baby doesn't end up being chased around in circles, running for his life, hanging on to a toy he's determined to keep in his hands for once. Shoot, if no one else mediates on his behalf, he just *has* to take matters into his own hands and let the playmate know the invasions must halt! Jeez Louise, the pickles we get ourselves into. By the time the assailant finally nabs your little chick, he's fed up beyond control and doesn't know what to do other than scream.

With years of cushion and other kids to raise (and kick you to shreds), you may be able to look back on it and admire the aggressor's tenacity. But in the Mommy-rookie moment, objectivity takes a hike. Being fairly new at this bickering business, our hysteria level is right in check with the victim. My gosh! The situation is untenable; our little lamb is so upset – and we let it happen! What a big fix, though! It's not *our* child on the offensive, so what are we supposed to do?

My Baby Has Been Violated!

What happens if another Mommy doesn't feel the need to address behavior you consider rude or aggressive? For hours on end I have sat my carcass down in the parenting section of many a bookstore looking for advice on what to do when other kids are mean to your own. If their Mommy doesn't seem to notice or care, what the heck are your options? Apparently, it's an incredibly taboo subject because I have yet to find a satisfactory answer.

I want to know the etiquette on toddler tussles. During a playdate or playgroup, can I actually intercede in a dispute where my child is prey, or do I rely on the Mommy of the aggressor? What if our ideas on the subject are not in agreement? Even if we do agree, it takes a very secure Mommy not to be offended if someone even intimates her child is anything less than angelic. Do I risk damaging or losing a friendship over some silly toddler fight? And what if, heaven help me, it's a relative or close friend whose child is the instigator? How on earth do I handle that situation?

One word to sum this up: Sticky. Every Mommy on the planet knows *her* child is not the one in violation of some arbitrary rule of etiquette. It's always some other heathen brat bullying our darlings. And if our perfect little muffin does happen to have an altercation with another, he's surely only defending himself! Even if someone replays actual video evidence of the event in which our sweet pumpkin pushes a little girl off a swing set, it's clearly because he learned that behavior from the resident bully! Besides, maybe that snot-nosed little girl was just being a swing hog. It happens!

I've met hundreds of Mommies. Very rarely do I run into the parent of a true toot who admits her precious is a bit on the aggressive side. Most of us think we wouldn't be worth our weight in changed diapers if we ever admitted such a thing. It's just too horrible! What kind of Mommy goes around telling other people that her baby is anything less than perfect? Yes, we are insanely protective of our offspring. However, there's no problem being ferocious with criticism of other people's aggressive tots! Heck, no. We bad-mouth away.

But to open your mouth to a Mommy' face and say you don't like her tot's behavior...Yikes. It's nearly impossible to avoid offending her, even if her little rug rat is running amok in your own home. Every Mommy has her own ideas on how to raise children, and there's nothing wrong with diverse approaches. But to tell a Mommy that your opinion is different than hers, especially when *your* darling has just been battered by *her* darling, is just asking for a catfight.

Heading Off Trouble During Playgroups and Playdates

1. Establish rules. In a more formal playgroup setting, establish rules. The guidelines should be the same for all houses, parks, or meeting places. If you vary the rules depending on which Mommy is more tolerant of having her home demolished, then it's too confusing for the kids and other Mommies. Keep the policy consistent. Don't go overboard, but address the aggressive or questionable stuff: sharing, hitting, biting, kicking, tantrums, dropping off kids, "what to do if..." and supervision.

Put everything in writing and give everyone a copy of the regulations. If new Mommies join up, give them a copy as well and let them know ahead of time that following the rules is expected. By the way, if you think setting up structured rules is a bit over the top, remember that all professional childcare facilities and schools have similar guidelines. Rules are in place for the safety and well-being of all children involved. Call me obsessive if you want! Having personally been through playgroup nightmares, I'm telling you, it sucks. Avoid it, girlfriend, or you'll be up all night fretting over stupid social etiquette.

Although a structured set of rules is best, if you're like most Mommies, you'll have a playgroup with less stringent guidelines for play. When your sweetie is consistently badgered in an established playgroup with no set rules, you have a couple options. You can suggest that setting up some rules might be a good idea since you've seen some conflicts. Or, you can try to negotiate with the Mommy of the instigator. (Good luck.)

2. Keep it compatible. Mommies need to get along with Mommies, and little people need to get along with little people. Otherwise, the entire date will end up resembling a torture ride at a Halloween carnival. This guideline is especially important because you may end up being the sole supervisor of another Mommy's child. If her tot and your tot don't get along, you are literally cruisin' for a bruisin'.

There are times when two perfectly wonderful toddlers get together and bring out the worst in one or the other, or both. Recently witnessing a biting fracas at the park, I heard the mother of the biter insist her child hardly ever did that, and when he did, for some strange reason, it was always the same kid that he bit. My friend Kristy had a similar story regarding one particular child that her daughter Kate simply does not like. When the two are forced to play together, it makes the Mommies feel like referees in a boxing match. The children get around each other and turn into "little demons." (Kristy's words, not mine! I may be a blabbermouth, but not stupid enough to call my friend's kid a demon. Sheesh, if that ain't dynamite waiting to be lit...) For whatever reason, when thrown together, these children act so uncharacteristically stubborn, willful, ornery, and aggressive that playdates are simply a no-go. Lunch date spaghetti doesn't even get boiled before both Moms are drenched with sweat and exhausted from breaking up the battles.

3. Distract unfriendly friends. It's not uncommon for Mommies to take turns dropping their kids off at a friend's house for an hour or two. This frees one Mommy to run her five hundred errands and gives the host Mommy a break from constantly entertaining her own child. It's a fabulous relief when kids play with each other and leave you alone for five minutes, but toddlers aren't exactly the most social and amiable creatures. When you force a toddler to spend an hour with another little human being who is just as devoid of manners, you'll have to face the inevitable clash. When the visitor initiates the scuffle and the Mommy isn't around to referee, my friend Holly has a quick and effective rule of thumb: **DISTRACT, DON'T DISCIPLINE.**

Generally speaking, when in a new environment, toddlers won't give you much trouble. They should respond nicely to "Oh, let's share, honey" or "Let's be careful please." If the visiting tot does something incredibly heinous, feel free to say in a normal voice, "we do not bite/hit/threaten other children/throw rocks at windows" or whatever, but don't take it upon yourself to give the child a time-out or any other form of punishment. If you do, you'd better be up to date on your CPR skills. You'll need to revive the other Mommy when she finds out and has a heart attack.

Distraction is the key when dealing with a visiting child. Do what you must to keep the visitor corralled until Mommy comes back. Then decide whether or not to continue the babysitting exchange with the Mommy. If the behavior is really out of character, cut the kiddo some slack. It's possible the poor critter is tired, getting sick, or even just having a bad day.

Dealing With "The Other Mommy"

When it comes to playgroups and dates, my girlfriends and I have learned the hard way that you have to be choosy about your kid's friends. Toddlers come wrapped in a package with their Mommy, and if she's not right up your alley, don't mess around making up your mind to beg off playdates. If you're a poor judge of character, beef up on the skill or you're in for some bizarre quandaries. I kid you not; there are some loon crazy Mommies out there.

Be wary or you'll get yourself into situations where you *have* to invite them to birthday parties, or you *have* to take their kid home from preschool. I'm telling you, it's a social nightmare. Learn to quickly recognize characteristics you don't like in other Mommies, and listen to your instincts. Don't bother brushing it off as a bad first impression or chalk it up to having a rotten day. If they're bitchy and neurotic on Tuesday, they'll probably be bitchy and neurotic on Friday.

Most Mommies recognize when their child gets out of control. But that potential thorn in your side is out there, so be on the lookout! I've interacted with tons of Mommies and yes, I've run into several who (a) I simply can't stand to be around, or (b) let their children be aggressive for unreasonable amounts of time. Obviously, it's not her intention to be impolite or blatantly disregard the feelings of others. More likely she's either distracted or simply overwhelmed. These Mommies want sympathy, not advice, and certainly not reprimands toward their child. Well, yoohoo! Sympathy only goes so far. When we dread getting together with the other party, we've had enough.

You may not agree with the other Mommy's approach to discipline, but the best response is to respect her views. No matter how ticked off, a wise Mommy will never boldly blurt out her opinions to another Mommy. When faced with a situation in which another child is consistently aggressive or cantankerous, your easy solutions are limited: You can bite your tongue and guide your child on how to handle the attacks, or you can remove your child from the presence of the offending toddler.

If you feel that separation is the best alternative, then you really only have three options: you can lie, be honest, or keep your mouth shut. Personally, I'd choose the last option and zip my perpetually footed mouth while backing off with my child in tow. Lying would entail making excuses as to why you can't get together once you find out that so-in-so's kid will be at the playgroup. Or giving so-in-so herself some long winded story about why you invited everyone else to your house except her little Boxing Betty. Being honest is much harder, but honorable, and leaves your integrity intact. However, trying to be honest can be like poking a hornet's nest, so be as nice and gentle as you can. Otherwise you might stir up hell's fury and end up stung.

Refrain from going into any gory or offensive detail. Just tell whomever you wish that your child and little Betty don't seem to get along very well and you think it best if you didn't get them together anymore. Betty's Mommy will push for specifics, but *keep the conversation very general.* Let her think you're an imaginative, ignorant, and judgmental fool if you must, but don't give in to her persistence at wanting to know exact circumstances. In actuality, if the behavior is that bad and you've had enough, the other Mommy is clearly in denial. Honey, she doesn't *really* want to know. Don't insist on telling her. Deep down, she may know the behavior's there, but if you force her to deal with it, you'll either get a hairy eyeball or a tongue-lashing-break-down-in-progress. Not good.

When Backing Out Won't Do: If you feel strongly that your child deserves to be in the playgroup just as much as Frank the Fighter, and you think Frank's Mommy needs to get an earful, then do what you wish, but hear me out first. Remember the old adage "I can say anything about my child but you can't say a word"? Heed the warning. Professionally, Dr. Chandler and I have been around too many aggressive kids to count, and it all comes back to parents. Most Mommies of consistently aggressive children will not be receptive no matter what you have to say, and ALL Mommies are bound to be defensive when someone else disciplines their child or brings up something even minutely unenthusiastic.

125

Parents and educators pursue Dr. Chandler like a rock star, begging for help with their out-of-control and aggressive kids. Yet even then, caregivers can be defensive and resistant to suggestions. So when it comes to regular old Mommy-to-Mommy issues, bite a hole in your lip before making any suggestions. Sometimes the Mommy will be as nice as a spring flower, asking you point-blank if there's a problem. Warning! Don't fall for it unless you're a great judge of character. Learn to sniff out fake nice or you'll have one fugly scene.

When out of good options and Tyrant Tyler needs to be ousted from the playgroup, do so quietly and discreetly. Don't go and gossip to everyone in the neighborhood. Just make an agreement with the other Mommies in the group to be honest with Tyler's Mommy and give her the "our kids don't seem to play well together" approach. You could even openly tell her that you and the other Mommies respect her hesitance to address the hitting, biting, or whatever, but you disagree and feel it best if she doesn't return with her child. Don't gang up on her. Chances are she's either highly defensive or highly fragile. Neither scenario stacks the cards in your favor by being cruel. Remember, if the kid is completely out of control, *there's a reason*. So be nice!

When the Lady Truly Needs Help...

Having the unfortunate luck to have dealt with some seriously psychotic and disturbed individuals (not all of them Mommies of young children), I've got to tell you, being completely honest doesn't always work. Sometimes you must fudge a bit to get the person moving on and out of your life. You can distinguish the truly "off" people by your gut feeling of truth and trust. Let me explain. Do they blatantly lie, make up ridiculous tales, or spread gossip? Do they use you or others to achieve their own selfish goals? Cheat? Treat others (even their children) cruelly? Expect special treatment for no good reason? Have you seen them blow up at anyone or get unreasonably aggressive or haughty? Do you have any doubts as to the safety and well-being of your child in their care? Make no mistake; these people need help. And you cannot provide it. So give it up and stay the heck away.

When you find yourself immersed in a relationship with someone before you realize you're seriously screwed, there *is* a way out. You can stop calling, make excuses, cut them out of your life, and let them think whatever they want. Just expect gossip and repercussions. If you're a strong person, you can handle it. OR, when there's no real polite or otherwise effective way of getting the person to peacefully bug off, you can put the onus on yourself. Make it your fault. *You* aren't good enough for them. *You* can't give them what they need. *Your* child just doesn't measure up to theirs. Whatever you dream up. It's technically dishonest, but sometimes the easiest way to deal with this type of personality. They have a desperate need for positive attention and absolutely hate it when you outdo them, try to prove them wrong, or disagree with their twisted logic. I'm not advising you to be a wuss; just be smart. Keep their ego intact and you'll be in for a lot less misery.

When the Other Mommy is a Family Member or Close Friend

It's bad enough when you have to deal with the unmanageable child of an acquaintance. Substitute it with a toddler you've known and loved since birth, and a Mommy you've been crazy about for ages, and you'll be popping antacids like the farty old man next door.

Family: For tooty family members you encounter on a regular basis, don't air your concerns. You'll gain nothing but family discord. Now, a strong personality can deal with this, so if you feel the need, go for it. Sometimes you have to stand your ground - and I get that. But the easiest way to handle this situation is to glue yourself to your child and supervise his play at family gatherings. It may mean tearing yourself away from the adults and missing out on the family gossip, but if cousin Chloe is just waiting for the opportunity to knock your kid silly as soon as you turn your back, you have to keep your eye on cousin Chloe.

When you maintain a consistent presence, you can offer your skills as a professional referee just as soon as the board books start flying.

Friends: Now, where close friends are concerned, it's different. First assess the friendship you have with this person. Is the Mommy someone you adore? Will she help you grow? Does she add joy to your life or do you find yourself worried about interactions with her? Next, consider whether or not the kids are compatible. If you are absolutely certain the friendship is strong, then toddler compatibility may be the root of the problem. Your anxieties over the behavior of her child could very well be reciprocated, so keep an open mind and don't judge her kid when yours could be just as wild and crazy. When your distress is strictly limited to the behavior of the toddler(s) in question, then separation is the best bet. Or you could always continue seeing each other, but keep your opinions and concerns bottled and wait out the tumultuous times. Let your children get through the toddler years and see if the situation improves.

Some experts advise that when the Mommy of the offender is a close friend, you should tell her that while your kids don't seem to be a good playdate match, you'd still like to get together with her kids-free. Now, you will have to forgive me as I rant about this particular piece of hooey. Yes, it's possible for this scenario to work, but you need to know the downside. Be careful when choosing this option.

In a broad sense, suggesting a kids-free friendship is no more potentially lethal to the relationship than any alternative, but you've got to know this is a loaded gun. No matter how delicately you approach the topic of separating your children, your friend could end up in a heap of tears. And that's not the end of it. She could quickly recover from the onslaught and mount an impressive defense, lighting in to your fat ass about daring to suggest her child isn't good enough for yours. Oh yes, it can get FUG-LY.

People are generally not keen on insinuations that their child is objectionable. Your friend may have a policy that stipulates, "If my child is not welcome, *I* am not welcome." Even when you mean nothing of the sort, if she feels you're clearly rejecting her child and it equates to rejection of her as well, then the damage is done. There's no going back, and you'll have to accept the consequences of broaching the subject.

There. I've fulfilled my responsibility in mentioning the kids-free friendship and pointing out the possible death sentence to your alliance. Having said that, if the friendship is secure and strong, then it just might work. It's conceivable your comrade will accept the differing parenting philosophies or agree that the kids' personalities are not compatible. After shaking hands on a solution, break out the champagne and toast your faithful buddy because you're darn lucky to have such a pal.

Will the Real Problem Please Stand Up? In all likelihood, the behavior of the child in question is not the real problem. Kids are kids and will, at some point or another, act discourteous, grab, yell, bite, hit, and basically act like grumpy pit vipers. So what? All of our kids do it. But when you get really irritated with the behavior of another Mommy's little waddle bug, step back and take a gander at the big picture.

Toddlers will only do what they get away with. Don't get mad at the short people in the scenario because they're just going about the business of being a toddler. Caregivers are the ones with sole responsibility in making sure the tot isn't constantly offensive to others. If the other Mommy truly doesn't feel the behavior is a big deal, then the entire problem becomes your own. You need to figure out whether you can accept her toddler's behavior...or not.

Between my three children, they have been yelled at, squeezed, pinched, bitten, swat, scratched, kicked, whacked, thieved, pushed, knocked over and ran over. Poppy has even gotten a nasty welt the size of a marble banged into the back of her head. And believe me; my children have certainly dished out their fair share of reciprocation. (Off the top of my head I recall Poppy dragging another child across the floor by her ponytail, and Mimi chomping a hole out of Poppy's arm over a red crayon. I think that counts as "bad".) However, with each incident, as long as the behavior was addressed, the other Mommies and I could have cared less. Everyone survived without permanent scarring because we maintained a sense of respect for each other. We were compatible and comfortable in our relationships.

True problems arise only when you get irritated or have disagreements with the Mommy herself. Keep this in mind when considering the risk of telling her your feelings. If you don't have a relationship built on mutual honesty, integrity, and respect, then what do you really have? If the relationship is sound, you shouldn't fear being honest with her or hesitant to ask her kid to follow your house rules. When you must deal with the behavior of another child in your own home, you should tell the other Mommy your house rule and ask if *she* would like to address it or if *you* should. **There should be no question as to whether the rule is valid or whether the rule will be followed.**

Being reserved or less than courteous about following your rules (believe me, it happens) is grounds for some serious relationship scrutiny. Balking at simple courtesies like being respectful to you, your child, and your home, may mean that the friendship isn't as friendly as you thought. Sure, you may have a fetish about having your white couch stained with cherry Kool-Aid, and you may be a bit protective of your Grandfather clock, but it's your house. You're allowed a sparkling white couch and crack-free glass clock. When another Mommy finds it unreasonable that drinks and lollipops stay in the kitchen and toy hammers stay off the clock, she has every right to smile kindly and deferentially pass up any offers to play at your house.

Responsibility – Looking at the Big Picture: I know I've painted an ugly picture, but before you go and get thoroughly irked at some Mommy for not taking responsibility for the behavior of her child, consider the situation. Most Mommies of unruly children are burned out and exhausted. They are tired beyond reason. They are sick to death of talking, yelling, spanking, time-outs, taking away privileges, and being embarrassed in public.

Honest Mommies of extremely aggressive toddlers will openly admit that the behavior you see is not limited to public displays, and not limited to other children. They have tearfully told me that they themselves are being hit, kicked, yelled at, spit on, and pushed around as well. These Mommies face incredibly intense emotions of humiliation, anger, confusion, and sadness. So when it comes to being hard on other Mommies for not assuming responsibility for her child's behavior, remember that most caring parents really are doing their best amidst a horribly difficult situation.

Chapter Six Review: What Did We Learn?

What to do when your child is picked on (Cry, of course! Just kidding!)

Three strategies to decrease fights during playdates and playgroups:

1. Establish Rules.

2. Keep it compatible.

3. Distract Unfriendly Friends.

How to tackle problems in playgroups that have no formal rules.

Strategies to deal with Mommies of aggressive toddlers.

What happens when the Mommy is a close friend or family member.

The real reason behind our aggravation with other toddlers.

Chapter Seven: Explosion!

Having survived many different tantrums with many different kids, it seems to me there are three types. The first type is the **Need tantrum**. These occur when kids have a need we haven't met, like food, rest, or emotional expectations. The second type is the **Overload tantrum**. Just like a computer, toddlers will blow up and crash when overloaded with too much information for their little minds to process. The third type is the **Demand tantrum**, which is the worst and hardest to deal with. Toddlers use this tantrum to get what they want and get it fast – for no other reason than it works.

Need and Overload Tantrums: Prevention is the Key

Need and Overload tantrums are fairly straightforward and easy to solve. (1) Make sure your child is fed and rested before you venture out with him, (2) be respectful of his schedule, and (3) don't crush his expectations.

Don't expect angelic behavior if you push it and drag him out when he's hungry or tired. When nap time rolls around, GO HOME and let him take a nap. Listen, he's not going to be Mr. Sit-Quiet-and-Peaceful in that stroller (torture chamber on wheels) when he's exhausted and needs a bed. And don't slap him with more stimulus by letting him take a spin on the Christmas train at the mall. Hells bells people! Overload! And as far as expectations, try your darndest to follow through with plans. If you've told him about it and he's excited, he might very well pitch a fit if plans change and he gets crushed.

What to do with Need or Overload Tantrums

So once the tantrum monster comes looking for blood, stop and take five seconds to assess if it's a Need or Overload tantrum.

Need Tantrum: Food/Rest: get your child some sleep or nourishment – fast. Do not reprimand or try to correct these tantrums, because the poor critters can't help it. Think of how you feel when you're starving or dog-tired. You're cranky, right? Toddlers are often having so much fun that they don't even realize how hungry or tired they are until it hits them like a brick. They're just going along in life, having a great time, and BAM! Those bodily needs take over their brain.

Exhausted or ravenous toddlers are irritable, sometimes furious. It's okay to tell them, "I need you to calm down - Mommy is getting your food," or "I know you're hungry, but we do not kick." Just don't punish a famished or tired toddler with a time-out. Solve the problem by feeding your child some nourishing food with protein or putting her to bed. Keep reassuring your little one that food (or sleep) will make her feel better.

Need Tantrums: Emotional Expectations: The best way to avoid these is to plan for contingencies. Remember my grocery cart story with Poppy? (Chapter 1) She wanted to ride in a special cart and I told her "yes." Then I changed plans and she threw a tantrum. In that situation, I should have said, "I'm not sure, honey. We'll see." That would have been the easiest way for me to change the (**A**) in my TAG. But as soon as I promised the special cart, her expectations were set.

Do your best to prepare your toddler for a possible change in plans. Go ahead and tell them the plan if you want but add the possibility of adjustment. Instead of "We're going to Jake's house to play after lunch," say, "As long as Jake is feeling well, we'll go to his house after lunch." Or you could say, "We'll try to go to Jake's house after lunch. Hopefully it will work out, because sometimes things change."

If plans end up changing, and your child is getting upset, that's the best time to guide him on what to do and what to say (ex: "I'm really mad! You said we could go!") Try to stop that tantrum before it happens.

Give him an outlet. Feelings of disappointment, anger, frustration, and upset are fine, but we cannot throw a tantrum. There are better ways to express those feelings. Guide your child on what to do and say. Be specific, and talk on their level.

When you find yourself up a creek with a disappointed, raging kid, hold to your guns and do not give in to the tantrum. The special cart tantrum was MY fault, but I still didn't give in. I missed the cues and opportunity to fix the problem and guide her on what to do and say, and I felt horrible about it. But once she got out of control, although I didn't punish her, I also didn't rearrange kids or go get a second cart so she could have her own. (Imagine pushing one cart and dragging the other at the same time. Navigational nightmare!)

She was way beyond happy. There was no reasoning with my child at that point, so I had to just let her finish. Besides, that was not an appropriate response. Toddlers have to learn that tantrums – no matter the reason – are not appropriate.

Unmet expectations let everyone down, adults too. Life happens, plans change, and disappointment is something we all must learn to deal with. That being the case, your child may still cry when he's let down, but hopefully it won't be a furious-raging-tantrum-cry.

Overload Tantrum: The reason for the tantrum is that your kid needs OUT and away from stimulus. I don't care if you've waited in anticipation for the big birthday party at Harold's Hamburger House for six weeks. He's not having fun, so what's the point? Get your toddler out of the mind-blowing situation and take him someplace quiet. If you're shopping, get out quick. Go outside and let him regain control. Stay by his side in case he needs you, and refrain from saying anything other than, "When you calm down, we can go back inside." And only say this about once every minute (an eternity in tantrum time).

135

Let me reiterate: **DO NOT TALK**. Your child is already on overload and doesn't need you filling his ears with more jumble. That one sentence (above), once a minute, is E-nough.

Once your child advances to the kicking/hitting stage, put him down someplace out of the way, and let him go ballistic. If he tries to deck you, take his arms or legs and say, "No". Let go and step aside. When he begins to wind down (which could take a good 10-15 minutes) and you see the rage begin to quiet, provide reassurance and comfort. Offer a hug if needed. Then go home. At this point, you could both use a rest.

If he doesn't stop in 10-15 minutes (this happens on occasion), figure out the best way to safely pick him up, and leave. Most kids can't sustain the violent kicking and hitting very long; muscles wear out. But they *can* go limp and keep screaming – which is (strategically speaking) the best way to give you continued trouble. However, the bottom line is that you are bigger. Use good judgment as far as your own physical needs, but do your best to get him in a car seat and be on your merry way. And girl, I know; groceries are in the basket, errands aren't finished, and time is short. It sucks. I've been there and feel your pain.

When all is said and done, remember: You're addressing the problem quite wonderfully by giving your child a time-out and taking him away from the source of the overload. Our job is to teach kids how to handle their emotions and actions when they get over-stimulated, stressed, and out of control. We must also meet needs to keep future detonations to a minimum.

Overload and Choices

Overload tantrums will also creep up if a child is presented with too many choices. Two and three-years-olds do not need, nor can they handle, more than <u>two</u> choices for any given activity or want. Your intention may be honorable in not wanting to force your will upon the child, but if you put him in situation after situation in which he's faced with too many choices, you're asking for overload. Your toddler's job is to enjoy life and learn by playing. Asking him to make a choice about something every five minutes is not fair. Don't make his brain work so hard.

When your toddler makes no attempt to make a polite request (i.e., "Blue dress today, Mommy?") then as the adult, you chose the dress for the day. If your little tootsie pop isn't happy with the selection, *then* give her two choices. When the two choices are met with an emphatic "No!" and pumpkin-poo decides to pitch a fit, tough noogies.

Throwing a tantrum for more choices actually means she needs <u>fewer choices and more limits</u>.

When toddlers get out of control, you choose for them. Period. You are the big person and you know what your child needs.

Demand Tantrums (Eeek!)

As the all-time bad guy and most horrible of fits, these tantrums can easily become a habit and excellent way for Jr. to break you down and make you concede to his every whim. Losing control of a child who makes Demand tantrums a negotiating tool will create a long, long trip down the parenting highway, girlfriend!

Demand tantrums are characterized by yelling, crying, wailing, going limp, or acting out by hitting, pushing, kicking, biting, thrashing about or attempting to tear away from you – when they don't get their way. Toddlers should certainly be allowed to feel anger, but violence and screaming are not appropriate.

With the first stomp and whine of a Demand tantrum, you must take control. Separate your child from the source of the demand and give him *no* attention or fun. If your little guy is playing and starts to tantrum because it's time to eat, take your toddler away from the toys, put him in an established spot (we'll talk about where in a minute) and proceed to **give him the opposite of the demand** – in this case, to continue playing.

If you are trying to put on his jacket for a trip to the park and he yells "No!" tell your child "Put on your jacket, or no park." If he doesn't cooperate, guess what? No park. No idle threats, Mommy. Squash it early. Follow through with your consequence. Toddlers have an excellent memory for what works. Give him the opposite of his demands, and he'll quickly figure out that the behavior isn't successful.

Direct consequences and time-outs are the best way to deal with Demand tantrums. Only use direct consequences if you're in a situation where the results are instant. The park is an excellent example. If you're putting on his jacket because you were specifically going to the park, and he doesn't cooperate, there is a direct and instant result: no park.

By the way, don't use this tactic if you have more than one kid who wants the park. Denying both kids a privilege over the behavior of one isn't fair. In this case, you'll have to figure out a different consequence - maybe sitting out for the first five minutes at the park while the other kid gets to play.

In order to be effective, the consequence has to be immediate. If you're trying to shop and tell your toddler, "Be quiet or you won't go to the park later" then it gives him nothing he CAN do, and the delayed consequence means diddly-squat. It won't work.

What Type of Tantrum is Taking Over?

To give yourself a heads-up on what type of tantrum you're dealing with, look at the frequency and time of day in which the tantrum beast starts to roar. If your toddler seems to have a meltdown every day after preschool, it may be a Need tantrum. For example, if your sweetie is asking to eat and acting tired just as soon as you pick her up from school, she could simply be starving and exhausted due to all the excitement and activity. If you have your child on a good schedule, you can easily meet needs by knowing when nap or mealtime is approaching.

Overload tantrums are more of a judgment call. If the kid makes like dynamite in the middle of a video arcade, it's not exactly a case for Sherlock Holmes. On the other hand, we Mommies don't always get red flags the size of a blimp, so we must take a look at the day or week our toddler has been through. This is all about the **A** in TAG. Figure out contributing factors. Take a look at increases in family stress. Are you distracted, sad, or edgy for some reason? Are you or Daddy having a difficult time at work? Kids pick up on these emotions!

Being tense, you may unknowingly treat your child differently. You could be ignoring or yelling without realizing it. A toddler can get anxious and overloaded when faced with strange and intense emotions from parents. One night not so long ago, I was ready to mash my kids' potatoes when my husband stepped in and said, "Whhhooooaaa. *Calm down.*" Good thing he did; I had no idea I was being such an ass. My dinner that night was a glass of wine and Tylenol, and only two whole days later did I realize it was dadgum PMS making me crazed.

Other stressors could be illness, trips out of town, change in homes, jobs, childcare, or even a death in the family. Also, new siblings most definitely bring on Overload tantrums! Think of how traumatic it is for a two or three-year-old to realize a miniature, unsightly, and annoying creature has invaded their home and stolen Mommy and Daddy's attention. Horrible, stinky, mangy little rat taking over the household — no fair! Complain to management, ASAP!

For the draining Demand tantrums, look at frequency. Frightful daily explosions? Yep. Demand. Another subtle hint is a toddler who is generally severe with everyday "requests" and insists you vacuum the carpet, fetch the neighbor's cat for him to play with, or go outside and mow the lawn RIGHT NOW! Even if he's not rolling on the floor wailing, if he won't take no for an answer, he's a Demand Tantrum kind of guy.

Time-Out

I happen to love the time-out concept because it's such a peaceful solution – a perfect example of how a technical (**P**) ("punishment" in TAG) should work. It's a break from an angering situation and a wonderful way to teach your child how to regain control during a Demand or Overload tantrum. *When used correctly*, I have yet to see a time-out fail.

A time-out can work wonders, but take note: time-out does not always solve the entire problem.

So plug in TAG.

When trying to decrease undesirable behavior, look at the reason for the outburst. What reaction (**C**) will stop or discourage the behavior? Time-out is a way for children to center themselves and regain control of their emotions. In and of itself, time-out is a total problem solver IF the behavior is for attention. When your toddler acts inappropriately simply to be noticed, and you put her in time-out to remove yourself and your attention, then you're addressing the underlying issue and choosing (**P**) in the ABC Guide. You're denying the child what she wants – your attention.

Many times however, time-out is just a way to get your child centered and calm so you can guide them on acceptable alternatives to their behavior. When your child gets out of control, a time-out may be appropriate, but afterward, tell/show them what you want to see instead. Model! Make sure you address the root of the behavior and guide your child on how to calm her emotions.

Occasionally, the single act of placing a child in time-out will enable you to tackle both issues of calming a toddler and addressing the underlying problem. For example, if little Waldo is grabbing and biting during a playdate, giving him a time-out serves to ease the intense emotion *and* address the biting. It forces the little guy to settle down, regain control, and recognize that when he bites or grabs, he cannot play with other children. It also serves as a direct consequence to the undesirable behavior.

Where to Put Toddlers During a Time-Out

The optimum place for time-out is somewhere that your toddler associates with peace and calm. You can use a corner in a hallway or even an open space in a large room. Just choose a place with no toys and nothing interesting to look at or do. Other recommended placements are a chair solely designated as the "time-out chair", the couch, or any other calming spot – just make sure it lacks charm and fun.

For children who sleep well and feel safe in their own bed, that's a great place to find solace. Just make sure they actually sleep in it at night. When kids aren't comfortable in the bed to begin with, sticking them there for time-out makes it the time-out bed, and there's nothing good about that. You may as well burn the thing and bury the ashes before you try and teach your kid to love his bed and sleep well in it.

The only place that's a big fat No-No in the etiquette of time-out is a closet. NEVER, EVER use a closet for a time-out. I know that large houses often have bedroom-size closets, but it just sounds too horrible. Never put a child in a closet. There is absolutely no need. Pick a non-closet location where you can sit your child down away from anything fun.

One and two-year-olds who aren't jailed in a climb-proof crib for time-out will boldly attempt any and all manner of escapism. Therefore, hover over your Houdini. Beds, cribs, and time-out chairs are useless if the kid won't stay put. So plant your feet in grabbing range and make him. When he crawls off the spot, put him back - eighty times if necessary! You can seriously spend 30 minutes just fetching your kid and replacing him for *one* measly time out.

But great balls of fire! If you are to this point, the kid obviously needs a good time-out. He doesn't listen to you, doesn't respect you, and he's not about to start until you get some gumption. Wake up and smell the coffee, girl! You deserve better and I'm about the only one on the planet who isn't afraid to say it. Besides, your kid is not happy. He's begging for limits. This is how you meet needs and make him happy!

Three-year-olds are generally easier to manage IF you're an effective disciplinarian. When they trust your word and will sit (relatively) still, you can put them down in a no-fun spot and walk away. Just stay within earshot and eyesight. You need to be vigilant so your child doesn't give you the toddler version of take-your-lesson-and-shove-it! Sticking an older toddler in a room full of toys and closing the door is just plain silly and useless. The vigilant ones will proceed in throwing baseballs and wooden puzzles at the door, or using cowboy boots to kick a hole in the wall. Never good. And when he's finished destroying the room, he's likely to get distracted by his new computer or ball pit and forget all about you and the point you were trying to make.

Initiating a Time-Out

When your child demonstrates a behavior worthy of time-out:

1. Tell her "Time-out. No hitting Mommy," (or whatever the infraction was).

2. Sit her down in the time-out spot and stand behind her.

3. No eye contact. Turn your head away if necessary.

4. NO talking. Don't say a word after the initial "no" statement.

5. If she tries to get up, sit her back down, and make her stay in time-out for one to two minutes.

As your child gets older and starts needing time-outs for knock-down-drag-out tantrums, use a designated time-out spot where you know she'll stay put, and walk away. Let her cool down.

Length of Time

A good rule of thumb for time-out is one minute for each year of age. For example, when not in full-swing tantrum, expect to leave your two-year-old in time-out for no longer than two minutes. This is a good gauge if your sweetie is not upset about the time-out and hasn't quite connected crime and punishment. You have to teach your child that time-out is not a special game Mommy is playing and you aren't sitting together to have fun. Say only, "No hitting." Do not look at her or give any attention other than sitting her back down after attempts to get up. When time is up, say again "No hitting" or "We do not hit," then go on with business as usual.

For any protests in which your child is positive the world is coming to an end, keep him in time-out until he regains composure or until you can no longer stand it. Be brave; tantrums loud enough to be heard halfway across the galaxy may take a while to wind down. Now, will you feel guilty leaving a screeching, crying, and out of control child in a crib or corner for up to fifteen minutes? You bet your pants you will. It's horrible.

Just remember, your solace in leaving your hysterical child in time-out until he recovers is that his attitude should turn to peaches and cream after he's allowed to fully recoup on his own. He'll be so much better off when you give him the guidance and time to cool down; it should outweigh any guilt. I say *should* – it might not, so be prepared and don't sap-out, girlfriend. Don't overdo the making up part or you'll be back to square one.

Children sometimes need ten or fifteen minutes to be alone. When secure in your love for them, they can release tension and regroup after a long or busy day. You could compare it to an adult wanting to sit quietly for fifteen minutes and enjoy a cup of tea or coffee. Everyone needs the occasional break – even toddlers.

Nobody Needs a Lecture

However you choose to approach tantrums, there's no need to go on and on about the behavior. Out of a five minute lecture to your child on why she can't hit her friend, she'll only hear, "Blah, blah, hit Jill, blah, Jill's Mommy, blah, blah, play, and BLAH!" Save your breath. Most beneficial is a simple statement of fact and consequence such as, "Time-out. We do not hit." Say it again when the time-out is over.

Don't start up with explanations when your child cries in protest, or guilt creeps in because you've taken away the brand new plastic dinosaur. A child on a tirade doesn't need you yakking in her ear about the inappropriate behavior. There is no reasoning with an out of control toddler. So be quiet!! No stimulus! Hush!

Lecturing toddlers on their behavior is useless and can end up pushing some major guilt buttons. As a speech therapist, I once put a preschooler in time-out with a beanbag and a blanket. No lengthy

144

explanations as to why he shouldn't have acted out; I simply stated the facts in a brief manner. Checking on him a few minutes later, he was quiet and looked ready to rejoin the group, so I said, "You can come and play with us whenever you're ready, John." He said, "Okay" and just sat there. Realizing he wanted more time alone, I let him be. Checking on him a few more minutes later, guess who was cuddled up and snoozing?

The sweet little guy was just exhausted and over-stimulated! Now, if I had made a huge ordeal about his behavior and jumped all over him for being inappropriate, how bad do you think I would have felt after seeing him lying there so peacefully?

Sometimes it's very hard to assess the reason behind a tantrum, and I try not to jump to conclusions, especially with a child who isn't mine. I don't know if they missed breakfast, I don't know if Mommy and Daddy are fighting, and I don't know if they've been up all night with sleep apnea and unable to breathe. They could be sick, or just need a hug and cuddle. State the facts simply and give yourself time to think about the "why". Toddlers need to know what is unacceptable, but you also need to feel good about your approach. No need to raise the guilt-o-meter!

Ignoring the Bad

Yeah, yeah, I've heard the rumors. Some experts propose ignoring or having a bored/neutral attitude about undesirable behavior. *Sometimes* this is appropriate. For example, when little Bobby conks his head on the wall for attention, you ignore him, driving home that he'll gain nothing but a headache. I also agree that some negative behaviors are present only to get a fantastic reaction out of the caregiver. In that case, keeping your calm, ignoring the act itself, and removing the child from the scene is the most appropriate solution.

Big "however" here, Mommy; ignoring ALL undesirable behavior is nonsensical. Call me crazy, but I'd say it's a tad unrealistic to have a bored or neutral attitude every time little Katie sinks her teeth into your arm and tears off a mighty chunk of warm flesh. It should be perfectly acceptable to bellow dramatically in severe pain and let her know in no uncertain terms, "We do not bite!!!"

Having a dispassionate attitude during times of outrage is boneheaded. Do you really think It's possible to put on a game face when Claire the Climber hikes her way to the tippy top of the highest storage closet in the house, frees Great-Great Grandma's antique crystal vase from five feet of bubble wrap, and proceeds to smash the lovely container to smithereens by pretending it's a piñata? God rest her soul, Great-Great Granny would have a cow right there in her grave if she knew her beautiful heirloom met such a violent and untimely death!

When it's Okay to Ignore the Bad: Let's utilize some common sense, shall we? The goal in ignoring bad behavior is to motivate children to do something different, right? You want positive attention, mister toddler? Then stop behaving like a baboon. Otherwise, I'm just going to act bored. Yawn. Ho hum. No big deal, my child's standing on the kitchen table, kicking plates around, knocking drinks over. So what. No attention for you, young man!

What an idealistic and peachy picture this is! But if the kid is inflicting some serious pain or damage, having a bored or impartial attitude will not help. It'll only give your little rascal the impression that you don't care if she tries to drown the cat in the toilet or smear your walls with finger paint and poo poo.

So here's the rule: When **B** in the Toddler ABC Guide equals pissed-off screams, and nobody else is affected, it's okay to ignore.

Example:

A = Child indicates wanting sweets; you say "no".

B = Child screams

C = You can:

> P = ignore the screams; turn your head away

> Or

> R = say, "Stop that now! Here - you can have one bite!"

Pissed-off screams are okay to ignore, UNLESS it's paired with other destructive behavior (throwing objects, kicking walls, hurting others). You also don't want screams in a public place – so don't ignore that. Implement some no-fun consequences.

Children need to be taught what is acceptable and not. Allow yourself the freedom to react as any offended person would. If little Rosie normally gets your attention by coming up and stomping your foot, don't just suck it up and hold in your yowl of pain. Ignore the stupid expert who told you to ignore it! Yell in agony all you want, girl. Kids need to learn the value of cooperation, deference, kindness, and respect. Don't ya think?

Chapter Seven Review: What Did We Learn?

Three types of tantrums and how to deal with them:

1. Need (Hungry, Tired, or Emotional Expectations)

2. Overload (Over-stimulated or too many choices)

3. Demand

How to prevent tantrums.

How to know when kids need fewer choices and more limits.

How to use time-out:

- Where to put them, how long, step-by-step how-to

- Time-out works wonders when used correctly

- Time out does not always solve the entire problem

No lectures!

The stupidity of ignoring or having a bored/neutral attitude.

When it's okay to ignore bad behavior.

Chapter Eight: Yelling, Biting, Bickering, and Hoarding

It's stupefying, exasperating, and downright exhausting when kids shriek, "No!" fifty times a day. But habitual yelling is only habitual when it works. So catch negative yelling early. Do NOT give in with a sigh and say, "Okay, you can play a little longer and then we'll go potty." Rewards for yelling and fussing will only perpetuate the problem. Do not reinforce negative behavior.

To reduce screeching in public places, catch and deal with earsplitting refusals to cooperate as early and often as possible – at home. When cooperation is nowhere in sight, use the home court advantage and let your child yell as much as he wants; just make sure the shouting is to no avail. Your toddler will probably still give you some deafening snubs in the most embarrassing public places, but hold fast and steady. Kids will pull on their memory bank of what you've done before, and if you're consistent, they'll have no reason to think shouting is any more beneficial in a church, restaurant, grocery store, museum, or mall.

Standard yells ("Nooo!" or "Don't want to!") can be a developmental stage, but can also get ugly quick. With novice yellers, simply tell your little shouter, "We do not yell at Mommy. You may talk nicely." Then proceed to do exactly what provoked the outburst:

Outburst: Little Lisa throws a fit because you request potty time before play?

Response: Take her to the bathroom for the task.

Outburst: All hell breaks loose when you present chicken strips for dinner?

Response: Too bad! Chicken or nothing.

If your toddler makes a nice request, feel free to oblige the initial appeal. When your sweetie politely asks to keep playing or delay tub time, then tell her, "Since you asked me so nicely, yes, you may play for three more minutes," or "You may go down the slide two more times, honey." Prepare your child for the transition by counting trips down the slide or giving continual updates as the minutes tick off. ("Two more minutes. One more minute.") Once time is up, it's up. Do not give in to repeated pleas to continue because children will ask until you say *no* – and mean it.

You have to provide guidance when transitioning, setting limits, and going about unwanted tasks. If you follow through with your promise to continue playing or allow your toddler to go on the slide "one more time," then you must also follow through with your promise that it stops there. Keeping your promise creates an atmosphere of security and teaches trust and cooperation.

Tricky Tricky

There are a couple of tricks that can work wonders encouraging cooperation, and they consist of giving your child a choice. When your toddler is repeatedly resistant to a request, drop the command format and present a question with two choices of activity.

Trick number one

Offer two positive choices. For example, when protesting a diaper change, ask your little one, "Would you like to hold the lotion or the powder while I change your diaper?" Or, if she throws a fit when it's time to clean up her books, refocus her attention with, "Which do you want to put away first, the fire truck book or the baby animal book?" Obviously, you vary the choices depending on the activity, but only offer two, and be gentle but firm in your assurance that the activity *will* indeed take place.

My friend Debi had a perfect situation in which she should have used this trick – and didn't. (Yes, it got ugly.) Debi had a lunch date with a friend and had to take along her son, Cole. She started out by enthusiastically asking Cole "Would you like to go to lunch with Mommy?" Cole was agreeable and excited – right up until Debi told him to put his shoes on. Cole happens to hate shoes, going to great lengths to keep them off his feet. So what happened? Debi and Cole went ten rounds with "Do you want to go with Mommy?" "YYYYEEESSS!!" "Then you need to put your shoes on." "NNOOOOOO!!!"

Debi could have avoided the entire fiasco by starting off the conversation with, "Okay! We're going to lunch now and you have to put your shoes on. Would you like boots or tennies?" Instead, she started off by giving Cole a choice in whether or not he wanted to go. This was a faux pas because in actuality, there was no choice. He was going, and shoes were part of the deal.

Blunder #2: missing the hint that the shoe argument was going nowhere. When going around in circles, you need to change course! By offering a positive choice, she could have given him some control – just a bit of leverage in his need to feel autonomous. Yes, it can still backfire; he can still refuse both pairs. In that case, Mommy needs to make an executive decision; pick a pair of shoes, and his feet go in. End of story.

Trick number two

If the positive choice method fails, trick number two is an option: Make one choice desirable to you and one choice *un*desirable to your kiddy, like a time-out. Example: "Do you want a time-out, or do you want to put the markers away?" When you use a calm and completely matter-of-fact tone of voice, your children will think the mere idea of having a choice is just groovy, and may cooperate with astonishing frequency.

My friend Kristy had an incident where her daughter Kate was resisting taking her nightly bath. Kristy restated three times "Kate, it's time for your bath" and repeatedly got three adamant replies of "No!" Giving up the command format, she asked, "Do you want a bath or would you rather go straight to bed?" Kate stopped, thought about it and said, "Kate want a bath."

Word of caution: when you give a negative alternative to a disobliging child, be prepared to respect the choice if your clever cookie calls your bet and chooses to forego a bath and go straight to bed. If your child is head to toe in dirt and french fry grease and you want the grime off before he hits the hay, don't offer the bed as an alternative. Think ahead. When you're pregnant, five centimeters dilated and laboring your eyeballs out, don't offer your three-year-old a time-out in lieu of donning a jacket so you can get your big belly to the hospital. Hoo-hoo and hee-hee breathing your way through three minutes of time-out only brings you three minutes closer to dropping a baby right there on your living room floor. Pick a "negative" option you're fairly sure your little genius will reject, but something you can live with should he actually choose it. Better yet, offer the adult solution and tell your child (in between contractions, of course), "You can put your jacket on NOW or Mommy will do it for you!"

But I Waaaannntttt It!!!!

Let's be totally honest. Our kids are spoiled silly. We buy them everything under the sun, so it's no wonder we get agonizing screams of, "I waaaannntttt it!" here and there. No big deal. We just have to get tough. So here it is again, Mommy...DO NOT GIVE IN to demands! You cannot surrender even once, or that's it. She'll remember what it takes. Feel free to be sympathetic – "I know you're upset because Mommy won't let you have the beautiful Barbie clothes. I understand it's very disappointing." Beyond that, they need to deal.

Knowledge of prior concessions will drive a toddler to utilize the weapon of persistence to influence your decision making process. Be prepared for some (initial) tantrums. If whining has historically motivated you to see things her way, she'll whine until you cave. Stay firm.

Here's how to proceed:

1. With the first hint of inexhaustible insistence, simply say, "We can't have that right now, honey" or "Not right now." Repeat the phrases as many times as you need.

2. Feel free to answer "no" and give a brief explanation to any _sweet_ negotiating retorts ("Have it later?"), but there's no need to explain anything if your child is getting out of control.

3. When meltdown begins, turn off the attention. No sympathetic looks, no apologies, and no consolations (like new shoes or a piece of gum – that's a bribe).

4. DO NOT reward the whining by giving in.

5. Use the distraction technique only if pumpkin is tired or hungry.

If you're going to distract, don't give little Charlie the exact item he's demanding. Rather, try convincing him your phone is much better than a cavity from the desired candy bar. Be consistent. He'll eventually realize he must either listen the first time you say no, or figure out some other way to get what he wants.

Look, I'm a sucker, too. Of course I've bribed my very own toddlers when the whimpers and complaints became unbearable. Indeedly-do, I've surrendered to protest to avoid a threatening headache and distracted my toddler by pulling a shiny bead necklace off a shelf. Just as soon as I finished tossing items into the shopping basket (and on top of my baby, I'm afraid) I made my bejeweled darling give up the prize by telling her, "Okay, we're all finished with the beads now!" I then put the miracle trinkets right back where I found them. (And obviously, not the only time I've done this, but a good example.)

Life will sometimes throw you too many stones to deal with at once, and you have the permission of all the Mushy Mommies on the planet to relent every once in a while and offer a consolation (okay, bribe) – as long as there are no tantrums involved. If Prince Volcano is threatening to make you collapse into a fit of sobs right there amongst the frozen pizzas, your official instruction is this: Give the little guy what he wants. Do what you need to make it through the shopping excursion without having a break down. Just do me one favor. Keep it together long enough to swing by the pharmacy and grab a pregnancy test on your way out. Once you get home, set up your royal subject with the five remote controls for your entire television and audio system, and go pee on that stick. If it's positive, we've found the source of the problem. If it's negative, take a Tylenol and call your therapist.

The smart way to head off undesirable antics is to reward cooperative behavior. Be consistent with verbal praise. Tell him how much you appreciate cooperation. Offer a great big hug and kiss. Buy your toddler an ice cream cone or favorite cookie every once in a while – totally out of the blue. Positive attention is a terrific motivator. Unpredictability and novelty greatly enhance reinforcement. He'll eventually come to the conclusion that positive attention is better than any toy in the store. Our hope is that it won't take our toddlers until adulthood to come to this realization, but we can only do so much.

Biters…Ouch!

I'm freaking out, I'm freaking out! Okay, no I'm not, no I'm not! Wait, no. Yes I am. Freaking out. *My child was just bittennnnn!!!* (This is me the first time. Cool as a cucumber.)

Okay...deep breath. Let's *aaa!!!* calm down. I have since learned that my kid won't morph into a vampire. Neither will yours. Biting is part of the life of a toddler; your kid will get bitten, and your kid will bite. It's practically etched in stone in the Toddler Book of Law.

Don't get me wrong. Biting is not excused just because it's a toddler-thing. The biter's intent is not always malicious, but gnawing on other humans is still a little on the impolite side. Younger toddlers (around 1 year) will slobber and chew on everything in visual range, exploring textures and taste. No biggie. BUT, if the chomping prize happens to be another kid's finger or nose...yowza.

When not a direct result of textural exploration or sensory stimulation, biting is a function of frustration or difficulty in communication. Either way, children need to know that sinking their teeth into living flesh is not an acceptable form of letting off steam or convincing another kid to give up the plastic monkey and animal sounds zoo. Biters bite because they need a way to express anger or aggravation. It's a toddler's very loud request for some guidance in the negotiation department.

As long as the chomping isn't chronic or vicious, it's just part of growing up. So here's the deal, Mommy. Don't get all panic ridden if your child occasionally bites or is bitten every once in a while. I've been bitten too many times to count, and I'm well aware of the colorful damage my kids can dish out and receive. But hey, we all carry on. The main points to remember are:

If your child bites: act contrite, not smug.

If your child is bitten: be gracious, not hysterical.

Our Baby as the Biter

When your child bites:

1) Address it immediately. Tell them, "NO biting! Biting hurts!"

2) Put them in time-out. Whatever the reason for biting, separation from the fun is a definite need. Plus, if overload is the culprit, departure is the answer.

3) Once the time-out is over, make your toddler apologize (if old enough) to the injured party, and spew out the apologies yourself.

4) Next, look at why your child decided to bite in the first place and address it.

5) Provide an alternative to the biting, depending on the reason (more on this below).

6) Plug in TAG and make sure you aren't reinforcing the behavior.

Example:

> A = Joey asks for a book and you say, "In a minute."
>
> B = Joey bites you
>
> C = You can:
>
>> P = Put Joey in time-out, leave the book on the shelf
>>
>> Or
>>
>> R = Put Joey in time-out, give him the book to read while there

Here's a different ABC:

> A = Playing at a friend's house; Joey gets stepped on
>
> B = Joey bites the stepper
>
> C = You can:
>
>> P = Remove him from play; put him in time-out
>>
>> Or
>>
>> R = Say, "Oh, Joey, honey, don't do that, it's not nice"; let him continue playing

DO NOT REINFORCE THE BITING. When you give him any part of the 'want' that sparked the bite, you have just reinforced the behavior. Tell him all day long not to bite and it'll go in one ear and out the other. You're letting him continue playing, and that's what he wanted. So TAG it. Figure out *why* Joey bit and which consequence will peacefully punish the behavior and make it stop.

Providing Alternatives:

1) Give specific guidance. You can't just say, "Don't do that again."

2) Tell him - in words he'll understand - exactly how you want him to express his frustration or impatience next time.

3) This is important. **Give him an alternative behavior** such as tugging your pant leg, stomping one foot, using words ("Please hurry"; "Don't do that!"; "Stop!") – whatever you can accept. He must have an outlet for the frustration; and *you* must pay attention, recognize it, and guide him.

4) The next step is to take the cue. Watch him like a hawk for further impending crunching episodes, and nip it before you have another munched victim. Step in and offer an appropriate solution to the problem. Repeat the alternative you've worked out as much as needed until he remembers and uses it appropriately. If biting continues in a social setting, pack up and leave the excitement. That's your cue that overload is in high gear.

Our Baby as Bitee

If your child is the victim of a little snapdragon, DON'T FREAK OUT. Resist the urge to slug the other Mommy or call an ambulance for your poor little darling. Etiquette calls for the Mommy of the biter to come running, apologize, and take care of the snapping turtle.

Tend to your wounded child with hugs, ice on the teeth marks, Neosporin, or whatever, but stay calm. The wound may look vicious and ugly, but kids are amazingly resilient. Your little one will probably forget all about the unpleasant episode after a lollipop. If the situation is just too horrible for you to endure without taking your injured child to the doctor, feel free to do so – but don't screech at the other Mommy to pay for it.

Hey, you *will* both live through it. The other Mommy will probably be just as horrified as you, so try to be gracious. Yes, I know you want to kick her in the shin for not paying better attention to her little heathen, but think how you would feel if the tables were turned. Most Mommies are sincere in their sympathy and apologies. Wouldn't you be?

Toddler Bickering

Toddler bickering is so common and frequent, you'd think we Mommies would take the hint and stop shoving our offspring into the snake pit and forcing them to be social. But no, we continually throw our docile babies in with the king cobras, forcing upon them our own communal needs. Playdates and preschool programs are sought out with religious fervor, so convinced we are that our children will have a splendid time with other similarly aged little creatures. The fact of the matter is, until toddlers reach about three or four years of age, they don't exactly play interactively. Rather, they tend to "parallel play" which means they'll play *among* other toddlers, but not necessarily *with* them.

To a toddler, parallel play does not mean space invaders. It does not call for other aliens to waddle into personal play space and proceed to interfere with, demolish, or otherwise wreak havoc on the current work in progress. Toddlers are fascinated by watching other toddlers, but often times the closest they get to initiating polite interaction is by snatching a toy.

Part of toddlerhood is learning how to interact with others, so if you happen to see a dispute, don't rush to save your little one too quickly. Sometimes it's beneficial to let children try to negotiate the problem on their own. If no fists or toys are flying and no tantrums seem inevitable, let the parties involved try to come to an agreement. Your green light to step in and mediate is when you anticipate imminent howling or boo boo's.

At that point, jump in and teach the kids how to behave in that particular situation. Let's say Jack is sitting on a book. Mary wants it. So she steps all over his blocks to get it. Show them how to resolve the issue peacefully and appropriately. "Jack, Mary doesn't mean to step on your blocks. She'd like the book you're sitting on. May she have it please?" If he cooperates, have Mary thank him and then thank them both for working out the problem in such a nice way.

Don't assume kids know how to act. Model, model, model! Demonstrate the correct behavior, and once children are old enough, have them repeat after you. When your toddler attempts to grab a toy from you, offer an alternative. Give a verbal example: "Tell Mommy, 'May I have the toy please?'" Always model desired language.

Along those same lines, don't assume toddlers know it's uncouth to bonk another kid on the head when they want the occupied toy. We must TELL and SHOW our children what's appropriate. "We do not hit other children on the head. Bobby is playing with the toy right now. You may choose something else to play with." Guide your child to another part of the room and get them engaged in another activity. If all else fails and you have no idea who started what, put the toy in a "time-out." That will usually settle any terribly hairy disputes.

Where are the Parents of that Brat?!

So what about the smart-mouthed little brat we always run into at the park or local pool who doesn't know manners from rocket science? It's definitely considered bickering, so how do we handle it? I'd say, "With gusto!" Make no bones about it. Tell the child calmly and firmly how he or she should be acting. I constantly find myself telling other kids, "We don't hit," or "Stop throwing rocks" when they're persistently throwing pebbles or bonking my kids on the head with their swim noodle. And why do I find myself frequently redirecting other kids? Because the parents of these little beasties are nowhere to be found.

You need not worry that some parent will rush up and start a cockfight. When it comes to lone kids, the behavior is generally quite typical because - obviously - the parents aren't around to straighten them up. And *if* by some miracle the parents actually happen to be present and paying attention, oddly enough, they're usually surprised and horrified to see some other parent telling their kid to back off. Only once has another parent even given notice that I told their kid to cut it out, and in that case, the parent immediately pounced on their child, letting him have it for being rotten.

160

If the parent of a little bully isn't around to defend your child and guide their own, be my guest in guiding the child yourself. Be nice, but firm. Parents who *are* present and paying attention deserve the benefit of the doubt, but not forever. (There's a 5-10 minute limit to this, people!) Hoping the attention-drifting parent will snap out of it and help, you can first make a (loud) general comment to the kid like, "Oh, let's be nice," but don't fully reprimand right off the bat. Give the caregiver a short lead-time to do the right thing. If they don't, you're good to provide full redirection: "Don't hit; Wait your turn; No running; Stop spitting." (And feel free to skip the correct niceties: "Saliva stays in your mouth." "Let's not push kids off the slide and break their legs." "We do not shoot kids with a BB gun, honey.") Keep your comments to behaviors that affect only your child. Sad, but true, most parents of consistently annoying kids are either ghosts or exhausted and whipped beyond reason. They don't walk around *telling* their kid to be snotty and hostile. They just don't have it in them to jump on the kids when they are.

Hoarding Hogs

I know, of course, hoarding toys is absolutely and completely normal. However, there is the rare child (ha!) who hoards to an extreme, getting a few kids and parents rather cheesed. If Jeremy has his eye on Daniel's fire truck, it's no fair for Daniel to put the toy behind him to "protect" it while he plays with something else. Or, if Daniel finishes playing with the fire truck and Jeremy rushes in for a turn, Daniel shouldn't race back to the truck and start a snatching match. Toys are for sharing and kids need to learn how to play nice. Daniel needs to give it up and let poor Jeremy have a turn.

Even if you don't think hoarding is such a terrible behavior, try to be respectful of other Mommies and their children. Being that no child is ever keen on sharing, you might find it a daily chore reminding your munchkin not to hoard. Something as trivial as a plastic ice cream cone can spur a screaming match worthy of a Hollywood horror. When it comes to hoarding, kids need us to step in and provide guidance. Otherwise, one little person will inevitably end up wrestled to the ground and stomped into hamburger meat.

Children will have a natural desire to hoard objects, especially their favorites. If your toddler has a couple of special toys, then by all means, allow her sole ownership. Put away the favorite fairy princess when you invite ten other girls over for a party, and don't allow big brother to take the favorite lovey or other stuffed animal unless you really want some catastrophic heart break. Let toddlers have a couple of favorites to call their own, and leave the rest for sharing.

Teach your child how to share and settle disputes when playing with others. Physically show your toddler how to act. Put a pause button on your conversation with another Mommy. Get up, go over to your child, and demonstrate what you expect. If you don't show them, they won't know!

A Quick Note About Siblings and Sharing

Let each of your children have a space of their own where they can work in peace and not get constantly interrupted by a sibling. Sharing is one thing, but toddlers need to learn respect for one another, even if it's a younger sibling (who doesn't know any better) pestering an older one. Don't berate your three-year-old for not sharing her puzzle pieces with baby brother when you know full well he'll promptly pop the pieces in his mouth and start munching.

Have your older child take big-kid activities to the kitchen table or a separate room in order to play in peace and avoid baby sister's grabby hands. If she has a certain toy she wants to play with alone (I'd bet Mrs. Potato Head falls into this category), allow her the luxury. Sharing is a must, yes, but it's also a must for your toddler to *get* respect if she's to learn to appreciate the value and reciprocate.

Sick Toddlers Are Cranky Toddlers!

Keep in mind that sick toddlers can be especially unruly. Making you wonder if she's been taking grumpy pills, your perfect pumpkin may be getting sick. Sore throats, stomach aches, ear infections, allergies, and headaches are all hard-to-express ailments. And really, we tend to forget how completely awful those symptoms feel unless we've recently been through it. When was the last time you had a nasty sore throat? What about a terrible cold that left your ears completely fluid-filled and pounding?

Teeth are a big issue. My neighbor Heather once cautiously asked if my kids had ever experienced diarrhea with teething. Hello! YES! Breathing a huge sigh of relief, Heather said her pediatrician firmly informed her that there's no evidence suggesting teething is associated with such Mommy-freaker-outers as fever and diarrhea. Feeling foolish for adamantly believing the opposite to be true, Heather was immensely comforted with my snort of indignation and prompt report that her pediatrician's take on the matter was bunk. Even if you aren't paying close attention, common sense will eventually ring a bell when your child consistently pops up a tooth right after experiencing what you're sure is the flu.

Getting hysterical about my kids' teething behavior and physical symptoms is simply my M.O. Rushing perfectly healthy kids to the doctor under the pretence of imminent death is nothing for me. So is being thoroughly embarrassed when my doctor kindly informs me that no, my child isn't dying...just teething. Sporadic vomiting, diarrhea, lethargy, villainous behavior; all teeth related. I've lost count of how many times I get the urge to toss my children at these doctors and yell, "Yeah? If you think it's that simple of a problem, then YOU take care of her!" However, in my defense, the last time I rushed my child in for nothing (quite recently, I'm ashamed to say), the doctor kindly advised me not to feel bad. She once had a parent demand a CAT scan for her child, positive the little girl's horrific behavior was neurologic. But lo! Diagnosis? Teeth. So ha! I'm not the only desperate parent in this city.

It's all too easy to get lost in your own misery when having to deal with your kid's howling and acting up, but take a few moments to remember how agonizing it is to have something as simple as a throat infection. Toddlers have no way of knowing they'll actually live to see another pain-free day, so it's especially tough on them. Draw on your Mommy reserves of patience and kindness. Give sick toddlers extra love and attention.

If your toddler happens to be infectious and miserable, put on your nurse cap and keep your little patient at home in bed (or at least relatively still) in order to speed up recovery time. And refrain from dragging your poor little sickie out of the house. We Mommies love other tots, but feverish faces, croupy coughs, or anything green and flying is likely to make us shriek with fright as we run to the nearest pump of soap and bottle of disinfectant. As my friend Taylor puts it, when Poker Night rolls around to her house, "Kids are welcome, but leave the germs at home!"

Chapter Eight Review: What Did We Learn?

Yelling & Arguing:

- Why kids yell

- What to say and do

- When it's okay to oblige requests

- Two tricks to decrease arguing and protests

- Five steps to reduce the demanding "I waaaannnttt it!"

Biting:

- Why toddlers bite

- 6 simple steps to control biting

- Do not reinforce biting

- 4 steps to providing alternatives

- How to handle it when your child is bitten

Why toddlers bicker: when and how to intervene (Model, Tell, and Show).

What to do with "lone ranger" bratty kids (no parents around).

How to handle hoarding.

Life with Toddlers

Chapter Nine: Bedtime Blues

I don't know about you, but before having children, I was scared sleepless by people telling me, "Don't let your baby sleep with you! You'll never get them out of your bed!" Good grief! Are all prospective Mommies doomed to a life of getting your face punched and legs pummeled by a person no bigger than a dog? A quick poll of the Poker Mommies reveals the guess is fairly close to the norm; only two of us make our kids consistently sleep in their own beds. The rest can't, or don't feel the need, to get the kiddies out of the sacred Master Suite. To be sure, it certainly puts an interesting twist on married life. Completely bewildered that these Mommies still have young pups in their den, I posed the question with awe: when and *where* on earth do you have a little married fun if you're banned from your own love nest?

My Poker Mommy Carey answered that she and her husband never do the tango in their bed, even before Tessa came along. Other parts of the house serve them well. No hanky panky in the master bed – that's strictly for sleeping. And Teresa chimed in that nighttime wasn't prime time for her and hubby anyway, so it's not a huge deal for little Tanner to sleep with them.

Not at night? Not in their bed? I need more specifics! I'm not exactly a walking lingerie advertisement, but I'm also not a totally cold fish. The main thing is, a line is drawn in this house; there's no getting kicked out of my own bed in order to enjoy a bit of married life. It seems to me that Mommies let little ones invade the Master bed for one of two reasons: they like the comforting closeness, or they're too tired to fight. Both reasons boil down to one thing: YOU. If you want the kids out of your bed yet all efforts fail, it's probably your own darn fault. Stop it with your need to cuddle (because it's *your* need, not theirs), and stop it with being a pushover. Don't make me come over there and snatch your Starbucks to get your attention, girlfriend!

My friend Jennifer told me several months ago that she absolutely cannot let little Dean sleep with her. He'll be thrown off too much and get out of control. Skip ahead eight weeks; all it took for her foot to be kicked out of that firm place on the ground was Mommy being lonely because Daddy left town for a couple of days. Guess who is now the guest of honor in her bed? Yep, a friendly critter refusing to leave...

Why Bother?

Really now, what's the big deal? Why do children need to sleep in their own beds, and what on earth does that have to do with behavior and discipline? Basically, it all goes back to building trust and meeting needs to keep kids happy. Children who sleep well and independently are children who are easier to deal with during the day. Why? Because you've defined a need of theirs for proper sleep and you meet that need, keeping them happy.

And with all this sex talk, I don't know how you could have missed it, but lest we forget we have a mate in bed with us who might – just might – like some respect and time alone with you - or time alone, period? Sans kids? No interrupto? You know, it *is* possible this person doesn't like waking up to the smell of an eight pound, peed up diaper in their face. And by the way, when the heck were you *planning* on ditching the kids? When they're twelve? You'll freaking be divorced by then.

Now, it's one thing if your family co-sleeps and loves it. There are those who are gung ho. Fine. However, if you *want* your child to sleep independently, yet keep caving to bedtime demands, it brings us back to consistency and trust (and you being a pushover). Kids need to trust that when you make a rule, you stick with it. Constantly giving in to bedtime hassles teaches your child that you do not say what you mean or do what you say.

Apart from wanting your children to get proper sleep, you must insist your kids sleep independently for *you*. You need a break, and you need time alone. Perfectly wonderful parents can easily become crazed and resentful when the desires of children always come first. Hogging 100% of your waking attention, kids won't die if you cut back and make some time for yourself at night. In no way, shape, or form, are you a bad Mommy if you insist on some solitary sleep – even if you're only doing it to save your marriage. Your toddler's need for time and attention will end only when you sprout feathers and wings and fly to the ends of the earth. I'm telling you, it's never going to happen, and we parents will die of exhaustion before our kids ever willingly let us rest in peace.

Nipping the Sleeping Bug

Most Mommies believe the only way to nip the sleeping problem is to make your child cry it out, and by the time the little guy is old enough to fling himself over the crib rails and toddle through the door you've just closed, it's truly a losing battle. Heck, by the time he's protesting sleeping in the crib, there's usually another little soldier in the mix and Mommy and Daddy aren't getting enough zzz's as it is. Your need for sleep wins and it's too tempting to simply toss back your covers and mumble at him to hop in and be quiet.

Understand this Mommy; your child will never want to sleep alone until you teach him the value. You carried him for 40 weeks, and he'll continue the tradition for as long as you can stand it, or until he's tired of you and wants to move on to some younger chicks. Call me cruel and cold and whatever else rolls off your distressed tongue, but the babies need to sleep away from you. At some point anyway. Before they're teenagers.

Begin by putting your child on a schedule. Schedules make it infinitely easier to read needs and cries. When you have a basic daily routine, you can teach your toddler to sleep in his own bed, and have a better feeling about whether his cries indicate a true physical need ("I'm thirsty!") or if he simply wants your company.

Crying It Out

Even when they're on a great schedule, typical toddlers tend to wake up twelve times a night shrieking if they're too hot or cold, lost their water or had a bad dream. These issues are simple enough. Offer immediate comfort and sympathy, rescue lost sippy cups or binkies, and shoo away all closet monsters before sending your baby back to dreamland. Your real trouble, however, comes when the kid refuses to sleep at all and gets on a crying jag.

Crying it out is actually a learning process for your child. Although it feels awful for *you*, letting a child cry for a few minutes is really not such a bad thing. Kids need to learn how to put themselves to sleep. **Getting immediate attention for cries will only perpetuate getting immediate attention for cries** - a perfect (**R**) in our ABC Guide. It's a big, fat, never ending circle! Besides, your child is crying because she needs help and can't fall asleep on her own – so help her learn!

Method 1

If at all possible, start the process while a crib is still an option. It's likely that the younger your toddler is, the shorter duration she will cry before giving it up and going to sleep. There's a five-minute Ferber method that's been around forever, and here's the deal: it really does work. Quite honestly, it sucks, but it works. Look online for the Ferber method and follow it to a T, or use my version.

Here's how to proceed:

- Let your child cry for five minutes. Stand firm.

- Go in and quickly comfort. Offer a pat, back rub, kind words, or kiss. Do NOT pick him up. Leave.

- Repeat as needed; wait five minutes, go in and comfort.

- The next night, move it up to ten minutes and repeat the entire cycle until child falls asleep.

- Each night thereafter, keep adding five minutes.

OR:

- Implement the five-minute increases the first night.

- Wait five minutes before going in the first time

- Wait ten minutes, then fifteen, and so forth.

Whatever you do, *as long as you are consistent*, your child will eventually learn how to comfort herself and fall peacefully asleep. But you MUST increase the time each night (or all in the first night) until your child is sleeping through the entire night. Don't go pantywaist on me or you'll end up with a kid who'll sleep until 2 a.m., then wake up like clockwork because that's as far as you've gotten each night before giving up and letting him take over your bed.

Consistency is truly the key with this, because your toddler keeps a mental log of how long it takes your sleep-deranged self to drag butt into his bedroom. Some toddlers will be just as consistent as you are. In that case, since I'm not one to sugar coat an issue, it's going to be one hell of a battle of wills. It's up to you to tough it out longer than your toddler is willing to push. Whatever you do, you must hold out or you will have put your kid through agony for no good reason. He *will* remember your wish-wash attitude but will *not* remember the two days or two weeks you spent insisting he learn how to get a full night's rest.

Method 2

If you insist that suicide is a better choice than closing the door on a distressed child, then try this:

- Stay in the room with him; sit on a chair or the floor.

- Keep the lights off; 'be there' but don't do anything physical.

- No talking, touching, or eye contact.

- If he tries to get out of bed, get up and lay him back down: no talking or eye contact. Then go back to where you were.

- Stay there until he goes to sleep.

- Each night, move a little closer to the door until you are out of the room.

This method is just a different mental game – and probably sucks even more than the first because you literally have to *will* yourself to sit there in the dark and take the anguish. But at least you know he's safe, and he knows you're there. In this way, *as long as you do this correctly*, he will come to understand that you are there, but you aren't going to do anything, so he might as well go to sleep.

Do NOT, do not, do not (yes, it bears repeating!) turn on any stimulating lights, give him toys, *or give in because you can't take the crying anymore*. Be brave, or you will just make things worse.

If you can't take this, then don't do it. Use the other method so you can at least close the door and go call your mom, have your husband tie you to a chair, or drown yourself in chocolate (ahh, endorphins). Giving up and failing to follow through with this or any other method will stress your poor child even more. He won't know which way is up, down, or backwards, and you'll just add to the confusion.

When two weeks of trying and failing rolls around, and your child consistently cries for the entire allotted duration, then there may be more going on than just a sleep issue. Remember, there is always a reason for undesirable behavior.

If you are truly being consistent (in most cases, the parents are not!), yet your child refuses to put herself to sleep, then step back and consider daytime behavior as well. Is it undesirable? Are you reinforcing unwanted behavior? Are you meeting daytime needs effectively? Look at other factors as well. Is she sick? Stressed? Does she have faith in your promises? Has she been watching any scary movies or images on T.V.? Take note!

My friend Jennifer used to take note of outside circumstances (**A** in ABC) when her son misbehaved at daycare. She wrote down each time he got into trouble, noted the day of the week, the time, surrounding circumstances, and the caregiver. In doing so, she figured out that Dean consistently acted out when he missed his nap at daycare, or when his favorite teacher was absent. With this information, she was able to educate his caregivers on how to decrease the outbursts.

If attempts to get your child to sleep on her own aren't working, then you need to try another way to get your child's recipe right. Remember, there are certain ingredients that make her tick, and if your stew isn't coming out the way you expect, you need to change the ingredients you put in. Step back and take a look at the big picture. Stop, think, re-assess, and try again. The key is to _be consistent_ when you try something new. Give it time to work before throwing your hands up in surrender.

Escape!

Crawling out of "jail" or bed is common. So when you hear the pat-pat of little feet approaching, get up and march that baby right back into her room. If she pops up twelve times after you put her down, toddle the little ducky into her room and put her back to bed...twelve times. Or twenty. Or fifty. At some point, you MUST get tough. Insist your child stay in bed once you put her there. It's that simple. Do it in a loving way, but be adamant. Do not give in to pleas, do not reinforce the I-need-water-I-can't-sleep business, and do not bother engaging the demands. It won't work.

Truly, one - or even 2-3 three times a night is average and expected, but getting out of bed with twelve different lame requests...I mean, come on! If getting your child to sleep is this problematic, I'd bet my minivan that daytime behavior is an issue and your little darling is playing a give-me-attention game. Why? Because you give in and reinforce undesirable daytime behavior. Why should your child think the same behavior won't work at night?

When your child comes to you with obvious, attention-seeking requests, deny them. Take that knife jab to the heart and suck it up, because it's not cute; it's manipulation. Keep the discussion to a minimum. "No honey. It's time for bed." Then put her back to bed. Period. Think me harsh and barbaric all you want. I'm telling you, happy kids are the ones who get enough love and attention during the day, and good sleep at night.

Difficult as it is, you'll have to routinely deal with your child getting out of bed, wandering the halls at all hours, and sneaking into the master sleeping space with Mommy. You may even work your tail off getting bedtime down to a working science, yet still wake up a few mornings and be surprised to find a midget in bed with you. Toddlers being the stealth missiles they are, this will happen on occasion. And hey, wha'd'ya gonna do? In the meantime, be firm.

One of my friends will deny her daughter's request to join the adults at night, but offers morning cuddle time in Mommy's bed. Does her daughter ever take Mommy up on the offer? Of course not. Mommy knows the requests are just a ploy to stay up, so she offers a reasonable solution to her daughter's "distress" over the need to snuggle – thereby nixing the issue. Her consequence (C) is a true and loving deterrent/punishment because she does not give in to the undesirable behavior.

Now, if you really want to stop the wandering and keep your kiddo safe, there's always the gate-option. The downside is, if your child is potty training (or already a professional pottier), putting up a barrier means you must respond to yodels and lug yourself out of sleep to come and open the gate whenever Nature calls. But heck, who are we kidding? You'd be up anyway responding to the calls to help wipe her bottom.

Freaking out: Separation Anxiety

Freaking out when left alone can be a toddler's certified memorandum that (a) you're a sucker or (b) separation anxiety is a wee bit out of hand. If separation anxiety is truly the case (as opposed to your leg being yanked out of socket), you need to slowly work with your little guy and get him to love his own bed and trust that you won't leave forever when you walk out the door.

1. Give him time to play on his own during the day to foster independence. Teach him that he won't die if you leave the room.

2. Balance attention and independent play. Don't spend your existence living to please and entertain the darling. But don't ignore him either, insisting he entertain himself all day. Find a balance.

3. Be honest about limits and time frames. Keep your word and do what you say. Building trust in you is of utmost importance!

4. Independence Activity:

- Sit with your child as you normally do, then start to back off a bit.

- Leave the room for 15-30 seconds to 'do something' then come back and resume play with him.

- Do this a few times a day, increasing the time. And leave him be if he's playing nicely on his own!

- If he looks up and realizes you aren't there, pop your head in and say, "I'm right here." Go on as normal, even if he's crying hysterically. Console and give comfort, but don't act like you've left him out on a busy intersection. This allows needs to be met, but teaches a new reality; it's okay to be by yourself for two minutes.

When the Bed Freaks Him Out: If the bed itself is the source of angst (he acts like it's a hotplate) then he needs to actually play in the bed during the day.

1. Get him comfortable with the bed. Work up from a few minutes at a time. He needs to know that being put in bed is not a death sentence.

2. Play with him at first, then gradually get him to play on his own while sitting in bed.

3. Once he's comfortable on his own, let him be for several minutes. Then casually ask if he's ready to come with you to (i.e.) help make lunch. Gradually work up to the point where he spends longer periods of time playing on the bed, with or without you. Make the bed a happy place. The play should be fun.

4. Try not to wait until he freaks out before you let him down. When you wait until he realizes he should be wailing, then the bed is again

associated with negativity. Not the end of the world, but try to avoid it. Take him out while he still thinks life is just peachy.

5. Caution: If your child has never actually slept in his own bed, DO NOT use this adjustment time to start putting him there to sleep at night. Wait until he's comfortable in it, *then* give sleeping a try.

Have a Bedtime Routine – ALWAYS

It doesn't matter which method you choose, or what kind of problem you have; you need a bedtime routine and plan. Work out a routine because toddlers absolutely thrive on bedtime rituals. Once in place, STICK WITH IT, and make your child secure with the consistency.

Anticipate all wants (water, books, etc.) and have them ready. When bedtime comes, give your toddler a time frame as to how long you'll stay and read books, sing, or talk quietly. Set a timer if you need or tell her "Last song/book" to prepare her for the transition. When time is up, give her a big hug and kiss, and put her in bed.

Do NOT climb in bed or cuddle with her until she falls asleep. DO make sure your child has a favorite stuffed toy or other comforting object. Leave on a nightlight or closet light because the imagination of a toddler is a thing to behold. When you leave your toddler alone in her room, project your secure knowledge that she is safe and you love her. If you know or suspect your toddler is secure enough, yet she still throws a fit, use the same strategies as you would if it were during the day. TAG it and do not give in. Most likely the fit is to get attention, and if you give her none, she will eventually realize the tactic doesn't work anymore.

Overtired, Overstimulated: In assessing fits of fury when you leave the room, take into consideration if your child is over-tired or over-stimulated. If so, and he happens to still safely use a crib, put him to bed and leave him alone. Make the room dark (save that night light) and quiet, and let your toddler de-stress and wind down. He doesn't need you coming in and messing up the cycle, so let him be. If he's just starting to calm down and you open the door to check on him, it could startle the poor darling out of a perfectly wonderful state of drifting off and start the whole cycle over again.

When cribs aren't an option, proceed the same, but treat it as a time-out. There's a delicate balance to achieve when - praise the Lord and glory be - we realize our child is actually calming down and going to sleep on his own. Leave well enough alone! He's not tying sheets together, planning to open the window and repel down two stories to freedom. There's a degree of common sense to utilize (yes, I hear you whimpering, "He could be sick! He could be hurt!") but we must balance it with letting our children learn to fall asleep on their own. Let's not distract them into psychosis.

Stick it Out: The magic solution in getting your child to love his own space is to **start as early as possible** and **be consistent!** Throwing in the towel after two months of progress with bedtime issues is a complete waste of 60 days. There will always be an early meeting or doctor's appointment in which you don't feel like arriving half dead. You need your sleep, I get that. But you are not solving any problems by giving up.

Midnight Owls

As soon as you teach your child to get to sleep on his own and stay asleep all night, it's inevitable you'll be thrown for a loop. If I weren't here to tell you in advance, you'd quickly find out for yourself that things continually change. No sooner do you have a nap schedule of noon everyday than your cooperative little angel refuses to nap at all for a week. No sooner do you triumph over the monstrous task of getting your toddler to eat vegetables than he reverts back to refusing anything but peanut butter and jellybeans.

This is an ongoing process, so don't be surprised when babydoll has been sleeping well for weeks at a time, yet you're shocked out of a perfectly sound slumber with shrieks of terror at two a.m. What on earth?! You've worked your tail off for months getting your child to sleep through the night, so what the heck is this? She's got to be dying! Fight or flight response - you grab the first weapon you find on your night table (a box of Kleenex or chapstick) and sprint down the hall like there's a boogey man you need to kill. I can't tell you how many times I've jolted awake, heart pounding, and rushed into Poppy's room whereupon she immediately ceased the murderous squawks and merrily signed, "Juice!"

Good, bad, or indifferent, here's where that sign language comes in! The first time this happened, I was thrilled she could actually communicate what she wanted. On the other hand, I wanted to screech, "No way! There's GOT to be a monster in here!" But no, all she wanted was some juice. Quickly deducing my neglected darling was sure to shrivel up from lack of fluid, we marched off to the kitchen to quench that poor, parched, baby throat.

The self-satisfied feeling of coming to the swift aid of your suffering child will carry you for a while. Only after being jerked out of R.E.M sleep for five nights in a row do you realize that maybe, just maybe, your midnight owl is playing you like a fiddle. Aside from the occasional ear infection or teething episode, sudden crying in the middle of the night (your baby, not you) is generally not cause for hitting the panic button.

While there's no need for your heart to leap right out of your chest, it's definitely cause for checking things out. Nightmares are quite common among toddlers, in which case, hugs and kisses are needed. Or, your bewildered love bug could've just thrown up and scared herself half to death. It's a good idea to eliminate illness, fever, or physical discomfort.

There's nothing worse than letting your child cry for forty-five minutes only to discover a diaper full of diarrhea. My own mother has been in a permanent state of remorse for leaving my sister to sob with a noxious diaper. Forty years later, Mom still feels guilty.

Illness and nightmares aside, toddlers may change things up a bit just to keep you confused and doting, so don't start a habit And don't let guilt rear its ugly head! If your gut tells you Margie the Merrymaker is getting up because she thinks there's a scheduled party in her crib, then don't feel guilty. Who the hell feels like making margaritas and shaking your bootie to Twinkle Twinkle Little Star in the middle of the night? Not me! Expecting a two a.m. apple juice cocktail is not cool. Gently inform your party animal that you're not a bartender, and she needs to go back to sleep.

Once you've rescued all loveys, checked for fever or poopy diaper, and established your angel isn't desiccated from thirst, your Mommy duty is complete. Be my guest in getting a blanket and sitting outside the nursery door to weep with heartache, but remember, she'll have to learn how to put herself back to sleep at some point.

Respecting the Need for Sleep

No saintly problem solver, my kids are just as normal as any others. Indulging in eight hours of uninterrupted sleep is a rare pleasure. I swear there are months on end when my insomniacs wake up five times a night with one upset or another. Through it all, I'm certain of one thing; the entire process of getting to sleep and staying asleep will be thrown into chaotic turmoil if I get them too far off their daily schedule. Kids love predictable schedules, and too much deviation stresses happily structured kiddos, throwing their sleep patterns into bedlam.

My friend Carey says her toddler will be pretty forgiving for one day of being off schedule, but two days straight, and you'll pay dearly. With shopping and running around on weekends, Mondays are not always smooth sailing for little Tessa. It's not uncommon for Tessa's sitter to scold Carey at Monday evening pick-up with an exasperated, "What did you *DO* to this child over the weekend?!"

When nap or bedtime rolls around, stop your shopping, socializing, and scurrying about, and go home. *You must provide consistency and respect if you want your child to cooperate with you.* It's bad enough these guys are stuck with you lugging them around or forcing them to entertain themselves in a stroller for hours at a time. How boring is that?

Unreasonable expectations loom behind the idea that toddlers should behave like angels when the need for quiet, uninterrupted sleep is snubbed. When your children are sleeping, don't run the vacuum, practice singing, go outside and mow the lawn (as if!), or test out the new stereo system. You might even turn on a fan or air filter in their room for some white noise. Life is not pleasant when children are yanked out of a perfectly good sleep by a circular saw, obnoxious motorcycle, or someone banging in a new roof. Some of us rather obsessed Mommies have been known to march down the street, shaking fists and shouting obscenities at anyone daring to wake up our babies.

Bye-Bye Bottle

None of my children have cheerfully endured the rite of passage to sippy cups, and I still count myself lucky in surviving the ordeal at all. Seeing the occasional three-year-old with a bottle or binky hanging from their mouth, I immediately sympathize with the Mommy. How can we, as the source of greatest comfort to our children, take away the most treasured item in the house?

Some would recommend letting toddlers keep the darned things for as long as they like. The need to have a nipple cemented to their tongue will eventually swagger and die, right? If you don't mind bottle duty and have no problem with your child keeping it, then by all means, let everyone else's well intentioned comments roll right off you.

However, if you're getting sweaty and anxious thinking about your nipple laden child taking the bottle out of his mouth only long enough to blow out four candles on his birthday cake, just prepare yourself for this mandatory battle. Believe me, the task may seem intimidating now, but once the ordeal is over, it'll be forgotten just as quickly as the location of your keys. Just go slow with the process, especially if your toddler is terribly fond of the bottle.

Farewell to Daytime Bottles

In order to hack the use of bottles during the day:

1. Get rid of all liquid in the bottle except milk. And don't heat it. If you or your child feels strongly about cold liquids, heat the milk to room temperature only, then slowly heat it up less and less to get them used to the temperature of cold milk.

2. Switch all non-milk liquids to regular cups or sippy cups. If need be, introduce one new drink in a sippy cup (or cup) per week. Give your child time to get used to all non-milk drinks in a cup of some sort.

3. When catastrophic cup-protests have ceased, start giving milk in a cup during the day. Start off presenting the milk during a meal, as toddlers will be more likely to accept it and less likely to simply toss the thing behind the couch and give you a dirty look for attempting to pull a fast one.

4. When meal-time milk in a sippy cup is routine, drop one bottle at a time, and give the cup of milk instead (i.e., before nap). If your child

throws a fit, too bad. You've provided her with an opportunity for milk. She can take it or leave it.

5. If you normally give your child a bottle of milk after lunch, start there and give the sippy cup instead. Don't give in and sheepishly fork over a bottle when your kid looks at you like you're pond scum and proceeds to have a tantrum. Stick to your guns.

6. Every few days, subtract one more bottle and present the milk in a sippy cup instead. You will eventually run out of bottles to get rid of and, viola! You've done it.

So Long, Nighttime Bottles

When it comes time to chuck the nighttime bottle, here's what you do: Substitute a sippy cup of milk instead.

1. First, make sure your dumpling is nice and comfortable with daytime milk in a cup.

2. Substitute a sippy cup for the bottle during the normal bedtime routine.

3. If you get the Heisman, offer a cup of milk before you even begin the nighttime ritual. Don't bring it into the bedroom. Once she's finished drinking, go about your normal bedtime routine.

When your child associates sitting in a rocking chair (or other special place) with getting a bottle, and the sippy cup just won't cut it, the choices are: **Milk in a cup or no milk at all.** If it's bottle or bust in the bedroom, respect the kid's choice. Give the option of milk before you even begin the nighttime ritual. Beyond that, your duty is done. You're a magnificent Mommy and your toddler won't starve.

It's a crapshoot whether your darling will balk at the idea of scrapping the bottle for a cup during her routine, but give it a whirl. It may not be received with a warm round of applause, but if it works, that counts as a check mark in the 'you're-a-great-Mommy' box.

To avoid hyperventilating and anxiety attacks, think ahead and be prepared for some upset. Introduce something new for your love bug to comfort himself with. A couple of weeks before you try to ax the nighttime bottle, get Jr. a new lovey or blanket with some silky binding. Give the lovey enough time to get a nice comforting smell (= shampoo, peanut butter, and a sprinkling of pee pee). By substituting one soothing item for another, you can reduce the anguish. I've also heard of a Mommy who literally took the shirt off of her back and gave it to her kid to sleep with. Smelling like "Mommy", the shirt gave her son great comfort.

Sippy cup Note: I'll be yelled at by all my speech therapist buddies if I don't comment on the detriment of sippy cups. Personally, I'm not so offended, but most SLP's go wild when you mention them. Sippy cups, especially with a stopper in place, require the kid to suck liquid out. This puts their tongue in a forward position. Then the kid starts talking with the spout still in their mouth, or the lazy tongue may decide to stay forward, and the kid learns to articulate sounds incorrectly because their tongue is in the wrong place. The same thing happens with pacifiers. Sucking, forward-placed tongues can make incorrect sounds, especially /s/.

Do I care so much? Well, yes and no. Of course I don't want my kid to need speech therapy for articulation. But I don't start growling at the mention of sippy cups because I'm dadgum tired of cleaning up messes. Kids NEVER hold cups upright. This means their carseat is crusted with dried milk and juice, on top of the ever-present crumb-fest of cheerios, raisins, and Gerber snacks. And not just carseats. Couches, carpet, clothes, animals, your feet. It never ends. And I'm sick of cleaning it up. So I refuse. I use sippy cups and I plug up the spout with a stopper. So there. If I offend you that much, feel free to follow us around and clean up the mess yourself. Because I'm DONE. I'll deal with the artic problem later.

What About Water in the Bottle?

Water is an option if you want to nix milk at night, but can't bring yourself to yank the sucking comfort from your kid. I was actually totally hip to this idea, convinced it would solve all my problems. That is, until I realized my children were more interested in making the bottle into a saltshaker. Foregoing the consoling pleasure of sucking, they'd have a blast dumping the bottle contents all over their beds, furniture, and clothes. Yea. Mommy duty being what it is, this means I must respond to the howling and get up in the middle of the night to change drenched sheets, blankies, and pajamas. So consider yourself warned on the shaking delights.

Generally speaking, toddlers aren't agreeable to having their milk switched for water out of the blue. To get him full and reduce objection, try giving your sweet pea a sippy cup of milk before you even put him to bed - then present a small bottle of water once you lay him down. Just hold your breath or dash out of the room quickly when baby Einstein puts two and two together and realizes that milk isn't what he's sucking out of that bottle.

You may discover that Mother Nature will occasionally throw you a bone. For example, my oldest daughter kicked her own habit of milk at night when she was all of fifteen months old. Getting a nasty stomach bug and yakking most of her intake, she was too frightened to drink a nighttime bottle of milk. From there, it was easy to switch to water in the bottle. Quickly tiring of cleaning up the gleeful mess, I up and stopped giving her the bottle and gave her a sippy cup of water to sleep with. She wasn't happy, but I was more determined than she was ticked. Needless to say, we both survived.

Water it Down: My last suggestion is one that never worked for me, but I'll tell you anyway, just to say I'm not biased. The rumor floating around (started by some crazy person) is that you can water down the milk bottle little by little. This way, you gradually end up with nothing but water in the bottle. Then, when you tire of airing out sheets every day, you gradually put less and less water in the bottle so that eventually your child is put to sleep by sucking air from an empty nipple.

I'm not quite sure how I feel about a toddler sucking air from a bottle, but it doesn't really matter. I never got past the watering-down part. My oldest daughter could sniff out that fake milk a mile away. Those bottles flew out of her crib as soon as she discovered the attempts at deception. And who could blame her? Watered down milk? YUCK!

So there you have it! There's plenty of choices in this chapter, and whether you feel they're harsh or not, they work. Stay consistent with these strategies to have happier, healthier kids. They sleep better, play better, and cooperate more. They have a need you fulfill. One of the most difficult tasks is doing things your kids object to or seem distressed over. But remember; YOU are the parent, not them. You know what's best. Behavior will tell you when you're off the mark. Listen to it. Observe. Change up your recipe. Plug in TAG and meet needs. Be brave, Mommy. We've all fallen flat on our asses too many times to count, but the important part is that we got up, tried again, and made it through. Woohoo!

Chapter Nine Review: What Did We Learn?

Why independent sleep is important.

Why toddlers cry so much at bedtime.

Two methods to deal with excessive crying.

How to get kids to bed and keep them there.

Step-by-step process to deal with separation anxiety.

The importance of a schedule, routine, and consistency.

What to do when kids are over-tired or over-stimulated.

The ongoing process of self-comforting.

6 steps to getting rid of daytime bottles.

3 steps to getting rid of nighttime bottles.

The problem with sippy cups (I don't have a problem!)

Chapter Ten: Developmental Skills List By Age

The following list will help you apply the training and knowledge you've obtained throughout the book and relate it to each developmental level. This list comprises more self-help and task performance abilities, along with the capacity to communicate needs and wants.

To help caregivers decrease frustration levels in toddlers, we need to know what kids are actually capable of regarding these skill sets. Remember the **A** in TAG? Can little Johnny actually be expected to neatly eat with a spoon? Are his motor skills on par or are we expecting too much? Are we setting up the situation for aggravation and failure? This list will help you determine what you should expect and when. Apply those skill sets to set up successful learning situations.

Important note: As a horribly defensive Mommy, I personally look at this list and start a check off in my head. Once I hit an age and task that don't match up with what *my* darlings can (or could) do, it's automatic "I'm a terrible mother!" So listen up. Do as I say and not as I do. This is a *basic* rundown of skills children can have at *around* the time they can have them, so don't use this as a panic indicator. There's nothing terribly scientific about this list, and nothing is written in stone. I simply spent several weeks out in the real world (ha!) observing kiddos, researching their skill levels at different ages, and interviewing every teacher and parent within shouting range.

I tried to be conservative with the list, but even so, give yourself a three to six-month leeway for each skill set. If your child just turned two and can't perform six activities listed under that age, don't hold your breath and pass out. Wait until he's two years *plus* three to six months, or 27-30 months. If, at that point, he still can't perform three of those skills, and it's bothering you to no end, check with other Mommies, go online and research, or call your pediatrician for reassurances. Most likely, it's not a big deal and he'll catch up.

Don't freak out if your child is a bit behind. The purpose of the list is to let you know what you can work on and feel good about. Every kid is different, every kid develops at their own pace, and every kid has areas they're good at and areas that need work. That's the way the cookie crumbles. We've provided this list to arm you with knowledge and alleviate guilt, not increase it!

How to Use This List

You have questions. Your child is acting up during certain tasks, lashing out in anger and hitting when you attempt to help him wash hands after using the potty. Can you really expect your 36-month-old to wash and dry his hands independently? For the answer, go down the list to **36-48 Months** and look under *SELF HELP*: TOILETING. (Sorry to use such an obnoxious word here – blame it on my therapy background. "Toileting" has always been the label.) Once you have confirmation that yes, he should be able to do this or at least be working on independence, you can apply Task Analysis to break the task into steps and provide appropriate prompts.

12-15 Months

Motor

> Starts cruising; holds onto furniture and walks

> May start/be walking; otherwise, can generally put one foot in front of the other as you hold one or two hands

> Able to wave bye bye; may still need gestural and verbal prompting

> May shake head 'no' when you say, 'no, no'

> Should be able to start learning and making signs or gestures to increase communication

Will only be able to make signs with gross motor or simple fine motor movements such as "bye-bye, eat, finished (modified), more, milk, sleep"

Turns pages of board book with or without physical prompts

Grabs at everything in reach

Speech/Communication

Should be able to correctly label and say mama or dada, possibly both

Points, signs, gestures, nods yes and/or no (may be inconsistent), cries, or uses words to indicate wants and dislikes

Can communicate need for sleep and food with signs or gestures

Consistently points to familiar objects using grunts or other vocalizations to request name/function

May have vocabulary of several words, although intelligibility most likely depends on context or familiar listener

Comprehension

Comprehension of phrases and requests is considerable, but language must be kept simple.

Understands simple routine questions or commands: Are you tired? Do you want to eat? No-no; no touch. Come here.

Self Help

Dressing:

> Helps with dressing by offering arm for shirt sleeve, sitting on your lap to put on socks and shoes, laying down when needing a diaper/pants change.

> Will get frustrated if dressing takes long or head gets stuck in shirt, etc.

Eating:

> Finger feeds self, although experiments with mashing, dropping, etc.

> Can introduce spoon; needs physical prompts for use; anticipate a mess

By 18 Months

Motor

Pulls toys (esp. if attached to a string)

Pushes (both hands) strollers, carts, laundry baskets, anything on wheels

Makes messes; empties drawers, baskets, bins, books off shelves, cabinet contents, etc.

Turn page of board book independently

Walks independently or with help

May walk backwards short distance without assistance

Climbs on furniture, playground equipment, chairs, etc.

Can put chips in a slot (Connect Four game, coins in piggy bank)

Imitates facial expressions and gross motor movements

Tries to turn doorknobs

Speech/Communication

Verbal vocabulary varies from a few words to several; not necessarily intelligible to unfamiliar listener (may consistently say 'da' for dog, 'ya-ya' for bye bye, etc.)

Can make requests: ask for object, person, or activity by signs, words, or gesture (pound on fridge, shake highchair, hand you cup, pat couch or chair wanting to sit)

Indicates dislike or refusal of object, person, food, or activity

Can understand and communicate need for sleep or food with words, signs, gestures, or vocalizations

Communicates when finished with meals or activities by words, gestures, or signs; may need verbal prompt, "Are you finished?"

Indicates wanting to know more about an object by gestures, words, signs, or vocalizations (pointing to tree and grunting)

May nod yes or no appropriately, consistently

Sign or verbally name familiar objects when asked, "What's this/that?"

If sign for 'more' is known, this will be a general sign to request everything until you teach specific signs to match wants/desires (book, eat, binky, cracker, etc.)

May begin using minimal phrases like 'daddy eat', 'mommy bye bye'; may sign these minimal phrases as well as, or instead of, talking

Tell you about pictures or objects with words, sign, or other gestures

Attempts to imitate new words/sounds being introduced; will watch your face carefully and attempt vocalizations

Comprehension

Follow 1 step directions/requests with use of gestural, verbal, or physical prompts (close the door, don't step in the grass, put it in the trash)

Comprehension increases with the simple, familiar, or routine (get off the couch, come with me, put the book away)

Can respond appropriately to "What do you want?" with sign, speech, or other gestures

Responds to routine questions (Are you ready to eat?) appropriately; i.e., walk to highchair, attempt to put on bib, nod yes

Understands 'no-no' and will either cooperate or deliberately touch to determine consistent response from caregiver

Understands 'give it to me' and 'spit it out'; generally knows they aren't supposed to have those object in hands or mouth

Can put toys away when requested (in bin or on shelf) with physical, gestural, and verbal prompts

Difficulty waiting to have needs met; does not understand/accept time concepts (wait, hold on, in a minute, it's coming, etc.)

Cognition

Anticipate adult actions in routine situations: put arm out for bracelet, point to buckle of car seat to unlatch, attempt to take off clothes for bath

Associates objects / knows what goes where; socks on feet, clothes in drawer, associate hat with matching outfit, lid on container, potty training seat on toilet, shoes in closet, etc.

Increase in problem solving skills; i.e., put coin in a shoe, then attempt to find coin by first feeling inside shoe with hand, then manipulating shoe different angles to look inside

Will seek adult attention or take hand and show/lead to engage help in problem solving

Correlates pictures from books or video to real objects

Knows when they've done something good; claps hands and looks for approval, accolades

Discovering cause and effect; will push, pull, squeeze, hit, or turn knobs on toys/objects to get response

Wants to do certain activities over and over; will indicate by vocalizations or signing 'more'

Self Help

Dressing:

> Can take off small items of clothing independently (hat, big necklace, socks); will help adults take off the rest by 'assuming the position' of removing shirt, shoes, pants, etc.

> Knows socks go on feet; will attempt to put on

> Tries to put on and take off shoes

Eating:

> Increase independence with use of spoon; less mess

> Uses sippy cup independently, but may spill on purpose for cause and effect; knows spilling is an 'uh-oh'

> Loves to be independent; hold own cup and drink with straw

> Easily communicates when finished with meals by words, gestures (hands you food or utensils), actions (playing with food), or signs; may need verbal prompt, "Are you finished?"

Toileting:

> Becoming aware of toileting issues; may say 'uh oh' when pees or poops out of diaper

General:

> Requires less constant, hands-on supervision in safe environment

Chew or suck on toothbrush; need physical prompts to brush teeth

Knows how to use combs/brush, but cannot neaten own hair

Social/Emotional

Beginning to understand 'mine'; will try to protect toys

Expresses (sometimes loudly) irritation and aggravation; will begin tantrum behavior: fitful cries/screaming, throwing head back, going limp, kicking

Begins to play independently for longer periods

Beginning to understand turn taking (peek-a-boo, throwing ball)

Understands when adult is upset, angry; child may also get upset and/or try to make up with hugs, pats, etc.

Starting to sympathize, take notice when another child cries; may offer comfort (given verbal and/or gestural prompts) with hugs, pats, etc.

By 24 Months

Motor

Drop, throw, or toss ball; aim may be off

Increasing balance: can kick, run/walk fast, get up stairs using feet (may require assistance), or by crawling independently

Can walk backward

Still pushing items/toys around house

Can stack descending sized rings on ring holder correctly

Grab small objects by pinching with thumb and index finger

Hold crayon or pen/pencil and scribble on paper (and everywhere else)

Speech/Communication

Speech varies per child anywhere from a few words to hundreds: if signing, can know 50-100+ signs and may pair with several verbalizations/words to increase communication

If verbal, can use 1-2 word phrases: daddy bye-bye, eat cheese, more milk, etc. May even start using 3 word phrases.

Clearly indicates needs/wants; easily frustrated if not understood. Will lead adult around pointing, gesturing, vocalizing, attempting to communicate.

Tell you about people, objects, sounds, and activities by gestures, words, signs, or vocalizations (brings you a book and verbalizes or signs pictures – i.e., 'bear' 'sleep')

Wants information about people, objects, sounds, and activities; i.e., hears a siren and says, "Truck? Uh oh!"

Very aware of self; uses words me, mine, my

"No!" used more frequently

Comprehension

Understands and follows 2 part directions in routine situations: 'Pick up the doll, put it in the bin.'

Can understand and express choice when given <u>one</u> option: Do you want milk? Do you want water?

Still cannot quite understand or express wants from verbal choice of two: Do you want milk or water?

Will retrieve familiar objects when requested (favorite book, toy, blanket, etc.)

Understands wide variety of questions and instructions: Are you ready for bed? No hitting. Let's wash hands. Find your shoes.

Answers some WH questions: What's wrong? What does the bird say? Where's mommy? Who's that?

Cognition

Remembers no-no's; clearly knows when doing something wrong and if caregivers are paying attention, but may not connect crime and punishment yet

Increasing expression of knowledge by pointing to objects, people, body parts, clothing, toys, etc. when asked "Show me the..." or "Where's the..." (Where's your bike? Show me the apple.)

Increasing ability to clean up room/toys with prompts

Knows where favorite or routine items are kept; shoes, cups, milk, blankets, binkies, etc., and will independently get them if possible

May seek approval before touching objects if caregivers are watching. May also deliberately touch or pick up 'no-no's' bringing it to you for consent or to determine consistent response from you

Look to caregivers for approval/disapproval, especially with new experiences

Problem solving skills increase; knowledge of prior experiences carries over to novel activities. Ex: Playing on new playground equipment, will be careful around high edges and stairs so as not to fall off

Consistently seek comfort (from blanket, milk bottle, binky, thumb, adult) when upset or tired. Coping skills mature, but frustrations increase as they are forced to conform to behavioral rules

Self Help

Dressing:

Able to help dress self with physical or gestural prompts (knows to put arms and legs in general direction of arm and leg holes)

Eating:

Uses straw independently; beginning to use cup with some spilling

Almost independent with spoon, but still experimenting with different foods/consistencies (applesauce vs. cereal vs. beans)

Toileting:

May become aware of toileting and be uncomfortable with wet/soiled pants; may also seek privacy (hide behind a chair) to poop in diaper

If language and toileting awareness is exceptional, can start potty training around 20 months. (Swear to goodness, I've seen them start at 13 months. Seriously. Panties and everything!)

Ability to communicate toileting needs varies greatly, prompting needed; some are ready for training pants, others could care less

May begin offering you a hand when washing and drying hands

General:

Can run toothbrush over teeth, but mainly tries to chew or suck on brush

Social/Emotional

Turn taking; peek-a-boo, rolling ball back and forth

Moods/needs swing; defiant, seeking independence one moment, hanging on to caregiver for comfort the next

Tantrum behavior increasing; will hit when frustrated, irritated, upset, or angry

When conflict occurs, often acts out physically and vocally (push, scream)

Watches other kids intently; copies actions or attempts to join play

24-36 Months

Motor

Will attempt to open gates, doors

Easily throw a small ball forward; roll small ball with about 50-60% accuracy

Loves to push carts, cars, etc.

Will push rocks, sand, etc., moving around with tools

Loves to shovel, pour, dump, fill, and transfer (rocks, sand) from one container/place to another.

Balance is better, but still a bit precarious; i.e., may lose balance attempting to get ball up/into (kiddie) basketball hoop, but can balance and walk a few steps on a 6-inch beam

Jump *up* with two feet 90-95%; jump *forward* with two feet 70%; jump *on* a specified spot 35%; jump *over* a Styrofoam noodle 25%

Can pedal tricycle with initial physical prompts, but mostly use feet to push self along

Kicks well

Runs, stops quick

Can run, jump, and climb well for short distances/heights; however, during an obstacle course, may trip frequently and need constant prompts

Tends to trip over shoes

Speech/Language

Uses 2-5 word sentences: "It's kinda cool outside." "She took my pail!" "I fall." "These are all mine."

Speech varies in intelligibility from around 25% (with strangers) to 100%

Response to questions often 1-2 words

Frequently use my, mine, me, I

Uses negations; no, not, can't, don't

Will cry and tell you about physical discomfort ("I hurt my finger!") but generally does not use words to express true 'feelings' (sad, angry, happy)

Tells you when something is wrong: "I got rocks in my pants." "I can't!" "It's not working!"

Expresses basic needs/wants well, although still cries when distressed (which can be often)

Comprehension

Concept of "one, just one, two" emerging; possible with prompts; i.e., child will say, "I got one," when they have an object/toy, but some have difficulty with the instruction "Give me just one."

Understands and uses "now"; i.e., child may say, "Are we gonna use that now?"

May or may not understand "later" but accepts adult explanations

Follows 2 step directions well: "Return the balls to the basket, then go back to your spot."

Needs LOTS of prompts for following directions, but does it well with instruction

Knows pronouns: I, you, he, she

Comprehension of quantifiers emerging: more, all, some

Understands "how many?" and will begin counting: "One, two, three, eight..."

Knows big/little

Knows up, down

With prompts knows: on, under, around, over, behind, in front of

Questionably understands possessives unrelated to self (our, his, her, yours), but accepts adult explanation

Answer WH questions: who, what, where:

Q: Who gave you those shoes?

A: Mommy gave me shoes.

Q: What kind of pizza is it?

A: Chocolate!

Q: What's the matter?

A: I don't want that.

Understands and responds to a vast range of simple sentences and questions:

Q: Are you okay?

A: I fall.

Q: How did you hurt your finger?

A: Don't know.

Q: What's wrong with your shoe?

A: My shoe's okay.

Responds to yes/no questions with verbal answer or action:

Question: Do you want to take your sweater off?

Response: Child starts taking sweater off or shakes head no.

Cognition

Attention span increasing; can participate in activity/instruction for up to 15-20 minutes with constant cues/prompts and physical activity

Knows 'severe' no-no's (stove, light sockets, stairs), but doesn't understand safety issue; curiosity may win out

Remembers significant events, but generally can't attach time (yesterday, today)

Recognize non-food items, but may continue to put them in mouth anyway

Associate similar objects/experiences and tell you; i.e., "You have glasses. My daddy has glasses. My grandma too."

Knows basic body parts (this will help when giving verbal prompts for dressing)

Problem solving: will keep at problems, attempting to resolve using alternate means to reach goal

Can infer directions and self correct. Ex: Child is asked to line up on a blue line, but doesn't do it. Teacher says, "Dan, is that a blue line you're on?" Child then gets on blue line.

May know up to 3 or more colors

Self Help

Dressing:

Can be independent taking off shoes (undo laces, Velcro, buckles). Many times child is *not* independent due to dexterity or too much parental intervention/help

Can remove socks

Can generally remove own pants and shirt, but won't if they're used to help

Eating:

May still need minimal help with spoon

May be using fork; expect some frustration

Needs constant prompts to clean up after eating, but will cooperate

Toileting:

Younger two's generally not potty trained and won't tell you when they need to go; need constant physical & verbal prompts to initiate and complete task

Older two's are better about expressing toileting needs

Washing/drying hands: may offer one hand, but generally need full prompts

General:

> May attempt to wipe own nose
>
> Consistently vocalize needs/wants, i.e., water, juice, body temperature (hot/cold), change of activity
>
> Often asks for help nonverbally; i.e., will come up with an untied shoe and say, "Shoe."
>
> Should be able to play independently, find things to do

Social/Emotional

> Younger two's parallel play, or play by themselves. As they approach 3, play more in groups of 2 and 3.
>
> Older 2's will play interactively; take turns (basketball)
>
> May join in on activity of others, but eventually vocalize possession "Hey, this is my castle." Others respond "No, not your castle."
>
> Often frustrated in group play; scream to express anger
>
> Watch other children intently
>
> Occasional shy bug does not want to participate in activities without Mom
>
> May continually seek out/play with a particular friend
>
> Engage another's attention to play ("Look, look, my ball.")
>
> Understands sharing and will occasionally fork over a toy/object/food

Very social; attempt to tell adults about their interests; will keep at it if not understood: "Look at this." "This is my drive [truck]."

Younger 2's still need adult comfort; prefer to stay close, hang out with adults to keep them nearby

Better at seeking appropriate comfort items/strategies when upset or tired (blanket, thumb, adult, or even words to express frustration)

Coping skills should increase dramatically by three, but frustrations will be great this year as they are forced to conform to behavioral rules

Begins to understand and vocalize rules of routine and behavior: "She's not standing." "The boy is spitting. That's not nice."

May try to give basic help; pat or hug child who's sad; ask for help for peers: "I don't know where her ball is."

Conflicts

Often try to resolve on own by taking desired object, pushing, or yelling, "no!"

Still learning conflict resolution, mostly with physical prompts and verbal instructions on how to resolve or need to wait for turn; follow adult intervention well ("Don't take that ball from him. Is there another one? Find it.")

Have some minimal problem solving/conflict resolution, i.e. run into each other on bikes, crash about 3 times before moving bike and going around other kid

Attempt to talk with each other but usually end up in frustration and "no!"

May cry when forced to share

Possessive: "My ball!"

Will finish with a toy, yet not want others to have it: "That's mine, okay?"

36-48 Months

Motor

Coloring: may still hold crayon with fist; less scribbling, more filling in picture, able to stay on page about 80% of the time

By end of year, will write name or at least first letter; working on letter recognition and formation

Draw circles, possibly other shapes

Can work on buckling, buttoning, and lacing; parental intervention often slows mastering

Can work puzzles of 9-12 pieces; enlist help of friend or adult if needed

Working on pouring/transferring liquid, beans, rice, etc. with different sized cups, spoons, utensils, tools

Uses slide

Mastering swinging; may need prompts

Working on pedaling a tricycle; still likes to push riding toys with feet

Balance on one foot

Balance still precarious when getting on objects/furniture

Jump with both feet off ground

Jump forward, on, and over (both feet) with approximately 20-50% accuracy (combined)

Can complete obstacle course with redirecting

Throw, bounce, and roll small ball

Work at pulling off back of stickers

Can pick up small pieces of paper

Can squeeze out little dots of glue with prompts

Speech/Language

Generally use 4-6 word sentences, but may verbalize anywhere from minimal to full, complete, simple sentences

If verbalizations are still minimal at this point, therapeutic intervention is probably necessary. However, until verbalizations and communication increase, they can still express needs appropriately, without frustration for routine tasks (depending on personality) using grunts, minimal speech, or gestures.

Intelligibility varies from 50–100%; may often depend on context

May not be able to express thoughts/questions clearly or following grammatical rules: "Which way I go now, guys?" [asking for rules to game]

Using more action verbs: 'saying, eating, making, going,' etc.

Will use past tense, but talk more in present, concentrating on current task or play: "I'm a racecar!" "You're messing it up!"

Asks questions frequently: where, what, how, why (LOTS of why questions)

Easily express needs/wants: "I'm finished." "I need more." "I can't do this; it's hard."

Pose when/where statements: "When I'm four, I get a party."

Personal pronouns: good use of 'me, my, mine,' but may still be mastering others ("Her poked me in my eye.")

Uses contractions: we're, I'm, won't, that's, etc.

Talks about recent experiences

Comprehension

Follow 2-3 step directions: "Take the cones, put them in the bucket, then go sit down."

Follow difficult, non-specific directions with less prompts: "Kelly, sit over in the middle. Amy, sit right here."

Follows inferred directions: "Where are you going? We're not done yet." (Child will sit back down)

Answer simple yes/no questions well

Answer complex yes/no questions (Can we jump up? Did we use two legs? Can we jump forward?) with about 50% accuracy

Understand complex questions and directions: "Can you pull the white part off the back of the sticker?" "Let's finish up. We

211

need to go to music class." "Move away from the door just a little bit."

Comprehension of all instructions/requests/questions increases with structured, familiar tasks.

Increased understanding of WH- questions (who, what, where, how, why) but may not be able to answer well

Q: What is that Charlie? A: It glows in the dark.

Often need prompts (more verbal than physical or gestural) to complete structured task correctly/appropriately: "Put the sticker on your paper, not the table."

Understanding of difficult tasks increases dramatically with use of physical prompts; may need to show child 2-3 times before they become independent

Can independently put activities/toys/crafts away when finished, if in routine

Know basic rules, when they (or others) do wrong, and consequences: "Is he going to time out?"

Increased understanding of safety rules, but often too curious or busy to obey or remember

Understands daily schedule, routine; anticipates activities

Easy to have conversations with to discuss problems, work out solutions

Cognition

Knows 3-5 colors

Count up to 10 fairly well

Beginning to understand 1 and 2 (just one, just two)

Understands concept of counting and quantifiers (more, all, some) as relates to needs: "I need 2 more."

Right/left still difficult concept

Recognize and name some shapes

Knows big, little

Time concepts emerging, mastering: *today*, *almost*, *when*: "I'm almost done." "When will my Mommy be here?" "She's almost here!" "I want to do play doh today."

Asks questions about what happens next/future activities: "Are we going outside?" "When'll we carve a pumpkin?"

Can relay future activities: "I'm gonna have a Dora party!"

Still doesn't understand *yesterday* well, unless something significant happened

Understand abstract concepts with prior experience and can empathize: when discussing peanut butter stuck on roof of mouth, child says, "Sometimes I eat cookie and that happens."

Knows name and possibly where they live

Understands differences between girl/boy

Can distinguish same/different in patterns, shapes, etc.

Knows on top, in front, behind, over, around, next to, and under with use of prompts

Attention to task increases to a good 15 minutes; may be restless during tasks, but most are focused

Enlist adult help to increase problem solving

Will tell you about potential harm: "I'm allergic to peanut butter."

May still attempt to eat non-food items for texture, sucking, chewing, etc.

Self Help

Dressing:

> Can undress and dress self; need prompts or assistance with buttons, buckles, snaps, zippers

> Learning to button/unbutton, snap, buckle, zip; many depend on adult, especially if always helped and never given practice

> Shoes/socks: Can take off independently; get socks right side in with time (and frustration); can get feet into shoes – may have difficulty manipulating tongue and Velcro; unable to tie laces

Toileting:

> 75% of kids are independent; 25% need constant physical, verbal, and gestural prompts to complete task

> Generally no accidents, but still need prompts with initiation ("It's time to go to the bathroom.")

Washing Hands:

Know and anticipate steps; may need prompts, but overall can rub hands with soap and rinse independently

Like to play in water when washing hands; need prompts to stop playing and complete task

Don't dry hands thoroughly

General:

Express general needs well: hungry, tired, want to go home, need help

Will clean up when given specific prompts/directions

Will wipe nose if handed a tissue, or will get tissue when prompted

Brushes teeth; may need prompts

Social/Emotional

More interactive play with peers; team up in groups of two

Attentive to other kids and adults; watch intently

Comfort others or give accolades: "It's okay - you're Mommy's almost here." "Good Tommy!"

Make up games with others, cooperate and negotiate rules

Pretend play, acting out cooking, being animals

Better about sharing; sometimes very giving, generous

Generally sits quietly when: Don't want to participate in an activity, finished with task, or waiting for turn or instructions.

May get up when finished with task and independently go to another task

Reads body language, facial expression, and vocal cues to determine moods/feelings of others; may need prompts and specific instructions on how to react ("He's very angry right now, so let's leave him alone.")

Sometimes impatient with needs/wants and expresses with repetition and increasing volume: "I need yellow, yellow, YELLOW!"

Looks for attention: "Look at all my colors!"

Increased need for attention if others get it and they don't: "I'm done too. Did I do good?"

Very social, engaging with adults; talks about interests: "Look at what I found!"

Talks about activities (i.e., carving a pumpkin) "We need a special tool." "It's icky! I'll need to wash hands."

Separation anxiety can still be an issue; better at expressing needs/wants: "I want my Mommy!"

Increase in coping skills to work through upsets, seek comfort object: "I need my blanket."

Knows rules, ask for permission, and report others not following protocol: "Can I color [now]?" "Do we have to share?" "They're had the wrong way." [They aren't doing it right.]

Conflicts

Still squabble over toys; younger 3's scream, hit, take, grab; need prompts to 'use words' to resolve conflicts

Older 3's use words more to resolve conflict, but may still resort to physical means and/or tattling:

- Child #1 gives child #2 a swat and says, "Hey, go away."

- Child #2 reports to adult, "They saying go away."

Increased problem solving; often need prompts; cooperates with adult strategies/instructions:

Adult: "Can you use your words to tell him to move?"

Child: "Please move."

Chapter Ten Review: What Did We Learn?

Developmental skills list for ages:

- 12-15 months

- By 18 months

- By 24 months

- 24-36 months

- 36-48 months

Includes the following skill sets:

- Motor

- Speech/Communication

- Comprehension

- Self help

- Cognition

- Social Emotional

- Conflict Resolution

Chapter Eleven: Be Your Best to Give Your Best

At some point, you have to step back and assess whether to keep plugging away and trying to answer the insistent bellows of your children, or whether you should stop, let them fuss and cry, and take a few moments to say, "I've had enough." By definition, kids are downright demanding. There's no getting around it, and they keep pushing until they find some limits. Part of our job is to assess *our* limits as well, and present those boundaries to our kids. Our children have no way of knowing how to respect our needs if we don't teach them.

We all want to do our job as Mommy and meet our kids' needs to the best of our ability, but our ability really does have limitations. When trying to have an adult conversation with our mates, yet the children are bawling, blubbering, or demanding, we simply cannot always address their needs first. We have needs too, and sometimes it's a matter of prioritizing. When my own toddlers act outrageous, I realize they're lacking something from me, but I can't meet 100% of their needs 100% of the time. I just don't stretch that far. And frankly, they'll freaking live if they have to wait for a fish cracker!

It's not realistic, or even possible, to make your kids happy _all_ the time. You have to find the balance between meeting needs and guiding children on what's appropriate and acceptable behavior. If you don't occasionally draw the line and let them bellyache, you'll never be able to sit down for an entire meal (and just WHO are we kidding here?), make a professional phone call, get through an entire magazine article in one sitting, talk to your best friend during a crisis, or - here it is again - find time to pee. As it is, we Mommies choke down most of our meals in all of three minutes. Even those few minutes are spent jumping up from our chairs; retrieving dropped spoons, refilling juice cups, and slicing more apples.

Mommy's Mood Sets the Stage: I don't know about your household, but for mine, great googly moogly if I'm not the one who sets the stage for everyone else. If I happen to be in a crappy mood, the whole family gets their pickle soured and panties bunched. This is the time when kid #1 decides to splatter coffee, #2 plants herself in the middle of the kitchen table and painstakingly demolishes the flower arrangement, and #3 won't shut up or let go of my leg for two measly seconds. Yep. House full of love.

The flip side of this mood-altering button is that when we Mommies are in good humor, everything tends to go smoothly. Am I right? We're better able to keep kids happy, get work done, and our husbands don't feel like trading us in on a new model. Most importantly, we can give our best to our children. When moods are good, we're patient and loving.

Recharging Yourself Is Imperative

You know the drill...exercise, eat right, find time alone, blah, blah, blah. I'm not about to tell you to eat rabbit food, or sweat your way to perfect abs and a bikini butt. However, there is something to be said for being a little selfish and prioritizing our physical and mental health. It makes you a better Mommy.

How? First, define and nurture a life outside of your family. And don't panic at the thought, because I know you love your family dearly. You don't have to ditch them. Just get a hobby like reading, sewing, gardening, scrapbooking, whatever. You don't necessarily have to leave home, but it's important to have some interests outside of entertaining and feeding you kids around the clock.

If you work outside the home and truly enjoy your job, you can certainly nurture that as an outside life. (By the way, don't ever feel guilty for enjoying your job, because some Mommies are truly better Mommies when they have fulfilling careers.) However, when your outside job is less than gratifying, don't worry. You can always find a hobby in which you can devote a couple of hours a week, after the kids go to sleep. Just choose something that makes you feel good. Do things you take pleasure in like shopping (you didn't hear that from me), remodeling the laundry room, watching movies, running, going to a wine tasting, painting, or taking piano lessons. Find your niche and fill it.

No, No! Not the "E" Word! Yes, my Mommy friend, the "E" word. I loathe bringing it up, but exercise is a great way to recharge. I used to wonder what idiot dreamed up the idea that exercising would actually give you more energy. Was this person certifiable? Doesn't exhaustion after a long day at work mean anything? Are you supposed to just summon up some phantom source of energy and motivation to get to the gym? Basically, the long and short answer is "yes." Justifications for avoiding exercise are plentiful even without kids in tow. Do what you must to motivate yourself because having kids certainly doesn't make you any less tired.

Contrary to my too-tired common sense, surprise of all surprises, exercise really does give you more energy (thus my apologies to the unknown person I thought was an idiot). Correct me if I'm wrong, but without a regular exercise routine, don't the ol' legs burn and lungs huff when we're trying to heave ourselves up a flight of stairs carrying a child? Pass me the oxygen! How truly pathetic we are. (Okay, I speak for myself). Exercise must be a priority, because the less you do it, the less you want to. When gym time slacks, you get too tired, and motivation takes a hike. BUT, the flip side is, the more you do it, the more you'll want to and the better you'll feel.

But I Have No Time!! I hear you. Of course you have no time. Hello! NONE of us do. But being a great Mommy, you are also capable of making the time. If you can make the time to take Jr. to the doctor

Life with Toddlers

when he's sick, pack up a nice healthy lunch for your budding preschool genius, or paint his room a different color every time he kicks a hole in the wall, you can carve out a few hours a week for yourself somewhere. As a Mommy, you are quite awesome at making time for other people, so put the talent to use for your own benefit. Learn to say "No" to volunteer stuff! Leave that to those chipper, scrawny Mommies with low stress and a housekeeper.

Look, all you have to do is get walking. Go to the gym or get a stroller and hike the neighborhood. Yes, I know the gym childcare is NA-STY and you loathe the buckets of snot and germs – and you have a perfect excuse not to walk outside during rain, snow, sleet, dark, cold, wind, or heat. Well honey, either get over it or get a treadmill. No, it's not lost on me that most of us get treadmills only to use them as storage space for Christmas wrapping and old clothes. But you've got to do *something!* Otherwise don't be surprised when a gallon of coffee is the only thing keeping you awake during the day. My friend Lisa bought herself a lifetime gym membership and promptly stopped going after four months. She now survives on candy bars and soda for lunch and drags her tired butt through every single day like she's hauling around a dead cow. Make any sense to you?

Stick your kid in a jogger or backpack and go for long walks on the weekend or days off. Put in a great CD and dance with them when you get home. Walk up and down the stairs holding them and singing. If you're standing trying to rock your baby to sleep, get a few squats in there. Get in some yoga, aerobics, or swimming with your kids. Put in a kiddie music video and jump around for thirty minutes – whatever!

Looking Good

Being our best doesn't necessarily mean we have to look our best, but when we do, we tend to feel better. So unless you're one of those disgustingly natural beauties, work in a dusting of powder, a little makeup, and quick iron to the hair. Knowing you look presentable will make you feel good. Unless you get pluck happy and create a highway in the middle of your left eyebrow, full make-up should only take all of five minutes. We feel a heck of a lot better about ourselves when we don't look like we've just had a mug shot taken.

Dress Up: I'm sure I won't get any arguments when I say that most of us perk up when we're decently dressed. If we bedeck ourselves like a hobo on a daily basis (I'm the Queen!), it doesn't do much to boost the self-esteem. Just like having comfortable and relatively sexy underwear (is it possible to clump the words "comfortable" and "sexy" together?), there's something about wearing a nice outfit that lifts the spirit and recharges you.

And look, I'm not talking about decking out just to dazzle your weekly playdate moms. That's stupid. I'm simply talking about getting rid of the sweats and baggy T's. Dress decent, but don't go overboard. Hard to hear, but we aren't seventeen anymore, Mommy. Sadly, most of us look ridiculous wearing hipster jeans and sheer shirts exposing our droopy belly buttons and tired knockers.

Now, I have to say, some of you guys just *have it*. I'm in carpool line last week, and this nightmare of a tanned, awesome-legged beauty struts by in her froo-froo, beachy-strapless print dress with platform heels. Well and good (even though I'm positive every mom in carpool wanted to throw up), but she was walking to school to pick her kid up. Walking. As in, from home. In those heels. Now, come on. Just a little footnote to those of you who have it going on: please refrain from letting your hair down, giving it a shake, and tootling past us fat-saps in carpool line with a wiggle and a smile. We cannot take that crap. Your compliment is our envy. Be happy with that and don't rub it in. As for the rest of us (oh ye of the spare tire and pear butt), don't go overboard with trend.

One last thing: Don't get stuck too far behind the times. Throw out your dated clothes and make room for new and more flattering threads. Once an outfit hits its second anniversary of hanging in lonely solitude at the back of your closet, consider it deadbeat and toss it. And as far as keeping all those "skinny clothes" you're determined to fit back into once you lose the baby fat...oh heavens, girlfriend. That's an entirely different issue that junks up your closet, causes more stress, and forces me to come over there and bark at you to put all that nonsense in a Goodwill bag. How many years has it been? They are *old* clothes, girly. Get new ones *when* you get skinny! Every month I whimper as I throw out some well-loved piece of clothing that makes me look like a sausage. Newsflash: We all get fat and lumpy. Move on.

Mommy Time

You don't necessarily have to leave the house to have time to yourself. Get your kid on a predictable schedule so you can work in a block of time for *you*. Have more than one kid? Get their naps coinciding and give yourself 90 minutes every day to do whatever you want. Take a nap, have a leisurely lunch, read, shower, sew, or watch a movie. These activities are nearly impossible to do when kiddos are awake and constantly needing hands-on attention. And don't use *your* time to do house work. That's a waste – and a rule! Your time is your time, period. When they're awake, you're working anyway. That's enough.

Time with Friends: Beg, borrow, or steal a babysitter so you can regroup and recharge. Get out with some friends and forget about home for two hours. I've been known to have a Winnie the Pooh song stuck in my head the whole way to a friend's house - only to vanish as I walked in the door. Then, as soon as my butt hit the seat of my car to leave, the song would pop right back in my head like a curse.

Finding time with friends enables you to recharge, vent about problems, and possibly roll with laughter. One Poker Night, Mandy made us wet our pants as she detailed a wonderfully scandalous marital fight. While stepping out of the shower, the quarrel began, and Mandy quickly found herself dripping wet and towel-less, stomping after her husband into the kitchen in order to keep up the banter. Going back and forth about Mandy leaving the backyard gate wide open, her husband Todd was doubly annoyed as Mandy dripped water all over the wood floor, remaining butt naked in front of all the bare windows. In an effort to end the quibble with firm finality, he mustered up a convincingly stern voice and growled, "You need to close the back gate!"

Just two seconds of silence. With a set jaw, narrowed eyes, and hands firmly planted on nude hips, she yelled, "Fine!" No sooner did he start to protest than she spun on her heels, yanked open the back door, and stomped across the yard in her birthday suit, smiling defiantly as she closed the back gate with gusto.

Seriously – the entertainment factor...oh my gosh! Put a little spin and laughter to an argument with your husband, or toddler behavior making you lose your marbles. Letting go of negative feelings allows you to open yourself up and get a better handle on your troubles, worries, or just plain exhaustion.

The Absentminded Club: Spending time with Mommy friends is a wonderful way to commiserate and escape the frustrations of memory loss and brain damage that goes along with having kids. You aren't the only one on the planet who loses your keys twice a week, drops your kid off at daycare sans diaper, and forgets what you're talking about mid sentence. Seriously, I have a friend who lost her milk. Yes, *milk*. In a gallon container. Lost it. Found it in the pantry a day later.

Letting Go for Longer Periods: It's not that we Mommies aren't frantic for a break. It's just the whole 'letting go' thing. IF by some miracle we could actually get away for a four-day vacation, how on earth could we sit on a beach, relax, get through an entire trashy novel, and cheerfully wave to our surfing husbands when all we'd really want to do is rush back to the hotel and call Grandma? We've got to make sure naps are being taken, loveys aren't lost, and emergency numbers are strategically placed all over the house. If Grandma takes a pee, the doctor's phone number should be taped on the wall in front of her in case she feels compelled to memorize.

Call me pessimistic, but I'm not sure there's ever a peaceful moment when you're a Mommy. The worry is so permanent that we just accept it and keep turning the pages of life. Being carefree is no longer a feasible option!

The first by-themselves-overnight-visit with family or friends is the worst. We Mommies could have a coronary for all the anxiety! Instead of enjoying our time off, what do we do? We spend not ONE moment relaxing, and become obsessed with how filthy the bathrooms are. Now is as good a time as any! Every toilet and tile must glisten! After our hands are raw and we reek of bleach, we throw ourselves on the floor of the nursery, weeping and hoping that absorbing our angel's smell will make our hearts stop aching.

The initial letting go is always dreadfully difficult, but once accomplished, it gets better. As a good Mommy, you will, of course, have the vicious tug of war we all have. But once you realize that your child will survive even if his oranges aren't sliced just the way he likes them, you will be able to let go, if only for a while. Use the extended time to catch up on big projects or relax and give your mate the full attention he (or she) deserves.

Hangin' in There

You know, some people insist on making it seem like life with toddlers is peachy-dandy all the time. They've got it down! And hey – maybe they do. More power to 'em. But most of us literally take it day by day.

There are some days (or weeks) in which we consider it categorically fantastic to simply make it to the end of the night without collapsing into sobs of self-pity and exhaustion. Forget a clean house. Forget a happy day. Sometimes it's all about getting through in one piece. Having toddlers is delightful, but at the same time, intense and grueling.

But at the end of the day, when all diapers are changed, blocks collected, army men put back together, and sippy cups retrieved from under the couch, breathe a deep sigh of relief. You've made it through another chaotic twenty-four hours. Savor it. Recall every single moment with your little angel. Burn those bright eyes, darling smile, and fantastic laugh into your brain. One of these days you'll wake up and realize you don't have to clean apple juice out of your carpet anymore. Your eyes will mist as you recall the little person who used to waddle around your house or gleefully smear spaghetti sauce into his hair. You'll desperately miss holding your little angel tight, getting a slobbery kiss, and hearing the words, "I lub ooo."

You may be exhausted, but take the time to cherish the life of your toddler. If today was rotten, try again tomorrow. Love your little guy with everything you've got and hang in there. You are a great Mommy. Times are rough now, but they will get better.

I may be fairly traumatized at the moment, but I do know I'll look back on these turbulent times and miss the pitter-patter of tiny feet, the desperate howls for blankies, and cheerful greetings of "Hi, Momma! How you feeling today, honey?" I'll long for the reaction of "wooow!" for everything from plastic french fries to a big red wagon. I'll miss playing with Poppy as she makes me "dinner" at her toy kitchen, asking if I'd like peanut butter on my cob of corn. And I'll recall with a smile the times when Mimi suffers a boo boo and whimpers, "I sorry!" or how she exclaims, "*No* eat soap!" every time we enter the bathroom.

Life with Toddlers

It may not seem like it now, but this time in your life will pass quickly enough. Each day is a gift, a challenge, and an opportunity. Make the best of each new sunrise, and the rewards will come. I know you can do it. After all, you're a Mommy!

Chapter Eleven Review: What Did We Learn?

How your mood sets the stage.

Why recharging yourself is important.

Basic recharging (exercise, hobbies) and how to find time.

How looking good makes us feel good – and be better Mommies.

Why time with friends is important.

Sharing the shame of child-induced memory loss.

The difficulty of initially "letting go" to recharge.

Author's Note

This is the second edition of Life with Toddlers. I wanted to scale it down, give more point-by-point information, and add an index. (My friend Carey read the first edition and screamed "Where's the index!? I need an index!") The index does not include every page where a word (i.e. behavior) is written, since many of the terms in this book are used too frequently! So I kept the index to main definitions or main points on the word/subject. Overall, hopefully the information will flow better and allow for quicker reading than the first edition - cuz dadgum, this thing is LONG!!

I wrote this book over an eight year period, so as you read along, at one point I've got two kids, then I've got three, or the oldest is two, then she's four...it can get confusing at times, and I apologize. I started writing this when my first child turned two and my second child was six months old. (I know what you're thinking, and YES, I was nuts...now you know why it took eight years!) But I truly felt like no one out there understood my pain. I had twelve different parenting books and they were 90% ridiculous. I really wanted to write a book while I was _actually raising_ toddlers – and put it out there to share with Mommies in the same boat. Once you get past toddlerhood, it's just like childbirth; you tend to forget how truly hard it can be. All the books I researched just didn't get that. So over 8 years of toddlerhood, I hope I conveyed the empathy, yet matured enough (does grey hair count?) to enlighten you with a tiny bit of wisdom as I struggled through mastering the art of parenting toddlers. And hey – I finally made it. Yesterday we went to the Texas State Fair, and for the first time ever, we didn't bring the stroller. I feel like such a grown up! (Now give me more cotton candy and fried butter!)

Also, please keep in mind: Beating around the bush is definitely not my style, but my writing is meant to be entertaining, not harsh or judgmental. Take it or leave it, but don't take it personal! You know I love ya, Mommy!

About the Authors

Michelle Smith is a Speech-Language Pathologist and mother of three. She has worked with a wide range of toddlers covering the spectrum from those with simple speech impairments to those with profound brain damage. Commingling her professional skills and personal experience, she truly understands the awesome task of balancing love and guidance. Her unique perspective and distinct voice allows her to empower discouraged caregivers with heart-felt, professional, and realistic advice.

Dr. Rita Chandler holds a Doctor of Philosophy in Educational Psychology with a focus on Early Childhood Special Education. She is a Board Certified Behavior Analyst specializing in Early Intensive Behavioral Intervention (EIBI) for young children with Pervasive Developmental Disorders. She works as a collaborating partner at Autism Behavior Consultants of Oklahoma, providing autism and behavioral consulting and training to individuals, school districts, and state agencies. She is an expert in Applied Behavior Analysis (ABA), a highly specialized and successful technique for changing human behavior. She loves Scottie dogs and spends her spare time spoiling her nieces and nephews – and of course, her three pooches: Kreela, Max, and Tucker.

Index

Index

Index

If you have a friend or relative that needs the fast version of *Life with Toddlers*, then the *Toddler ABC Guide to Discipline* is the answer.

Reviews for the *Toddler ABC Guide to Discipline*:

"I pick this book up and could immediately relate to the issues the author talks about. As a home-school dad I am always on the look out for quality materials that can greatly benefit and inspire both the parent and the child. Too many times I have heard parents ask "When is the best time to start positive instruction?". The answer is now, and this book is your road map." - **E.T. Pate**.

"This book is a quick and easy read for a busy mom. It gets the point across in a entertaining and informative way. It certainly made me rethink how to handle bad behavior. I loved the author's techniques because they are positive, very passive and they really work!!! I would highly recommend this book to all mom's and dad's." - **Sandy M.**

Brass, outspoken and witty, *Taboo Secrets of Pregnancy* dishes out practical advice and pee-in-your-pants fun like no one yet.

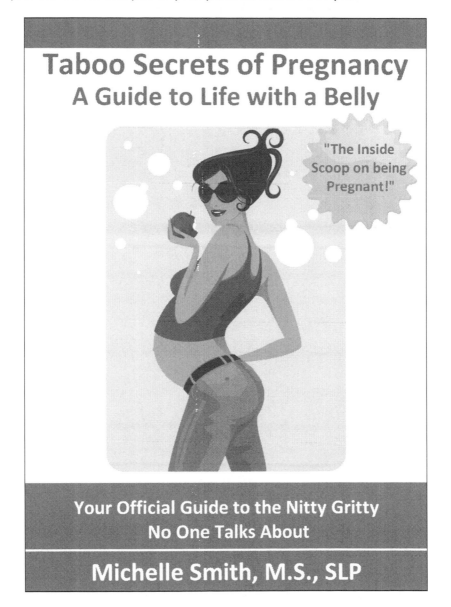

Taboo Secrets of Pregnancy
A Guide to Life with a Belly

"The Inside Scoop on being Pregnant!"

Your Official Guide to the Nitty Gritty No One Talks About

Michelle Smith, M.S., SLP

Join this pregnant mom of two as she journeys yet again through the rough and tumble life of a pregger. Boldly proclaiming taboo truths on those touchy subjects that books gloss over and doctors 'forget' to mention, this guide lets empathy roll in as the naked bum of truth is bared.

From gassy bellies and "fartle" (mercy alive!) to sprouting hairs in unmentionable places, *Taboo Secrets of Pregnancy* spells it out in no uncertain terms, and actually provides realistic guidance on what the blazes to do about it.

Just a few taboo topics are:

- Twenty Four Pounds of Boob, Comin' Through!

- Poop & Grapes (Bowels & Hemorrhoids)

- Puke-a-Rama (Brutal nausea)

- Bye Bye Thongs

- Don't Buy a Hot Pink Swimsuit

- The Art of Peeing in a Cup

- Varicose (or 'Very Gross') Veins

- Train to Grossville (Passing your plug)

Say goodbye to fragile advice and get ready to hear it like it is. Toughen up your delicate senses, girly! You're about to take a break from the technical tomes, and dive in for an adventure in gestating!

Reviews for the *Taboo Secrets of Pregnancy*:

"Great, VERY reassuring, and crazy funny!" - **Leslie**.

"Refreshing and hilarious - I laughed so hard I was crying!" - **Monica**.

Made in the USA
Lexington, KY
10 March 2013